I0104971

The Acadians

THE ACADIANS

Their Deportation and Wanderings

TOGETHER WITH A CONSIDERATION OF THE HISTORICAL BASIS
FOR LONGFELLOW'S POEM

EVANGELINE

*With extracts from the original documents bearing upon the subject, and illustrations
of scenes in and around Grand-Pré and Annapolis, Nova Scotia
" the Land of Evangeline."*

BY

GEORGE P. BIBLE, A.M.

A FIREBIRD PRESS BOOK

PELICAN PUBLISHING COMPANY
GRETNA 2014

Printed in the United States of America
Published by Pelican Publishing Company, Inc.
1000 Burmaster Street, Gretna, Louisiana 70053

PREFACE

If every book must have a preface, and every author an excuse for writing it, then we will briefly explain why this book asks for a hearing.

Every student of literature has read Longfellow's beautiful poem, " Evangeline," and generations yet unborn will read and re-read it with increasing interest as the years go by. Indeed, while lovers love and hearts are true, the story of Evangeline will never lose its charm.

With its historic setting, it will always enlist our sympathies and command our admiration for the loyalty, simplicity and self-sacrifice of these home-loving Acadian peasants. The reader naturally asks how much of the poem is historically true, and where he may find something more definite relating to this people, without searching through musty records, to find, here and there, bits of information upon the subject.

Our smaller histories merely mention the incident of their expulsion, and lack of space prevents their throwing any additional sidelight upon the subject. We have, therefore, compiled from the most recent and authentic sources, supplemented by a trip through that country, a brief sketch of the Acadian, his early struggles, his home life, cruel deportation, the confiscation of his property and destruction of his home; his treatment in exile and his wanderings in search of his kith and kin for twenty-five years following their separation. We have endeavored to give something of the life of his descendants as now found in the Madawaska country in the northeastern part of Maine and the adjacent parts of New Brunswick, on the St. John's River; on the shores of St. Mary's Bay, in Nova Scotia; and in the Teche country, in Louisiana.

We believe every reader of the poem will want to read this historical sketch, and we are sure every reader of the sketch will re-read with renewed interest the beautiful poem.

Our acknowledgment and sincere thanks are due to the Hon. C. H. Mouton, of Lafayette, Louisiana, and to Associate Justice of the Supreme Court, Joseph A. Breaux, of New Orleans, Louisiana, for valuable information furnished to the author concerning the Acadian of the Teche country, and for permission to publish extracts from their letters. The sketch of the wooden chest, a valuable heirloom of the family, was made by Mr. C. H. Mouton, a man over eighty years old at the time the sketch was made (1903).

To the Mouton ancestry may be correctly traced the original historic incident, which in after years gave Longfellow the basis for his " Evangeline." This accounts for the grave of the real Evangeline being located in the Teche country of the South, while the poet has given Philadelphia as the last resting place of his beautiful creation.

G. P. B.

PHILADELPHIA,
        May, 1906.

CONTENTS

CHAPTER I.

CHAPTER II.

CHAPTER III.

CHAPTER IV.

Contents.

9

CHAPTER V.

Grants to Charles La Tour and D'Aulnay-Charnisay by Louis XIII—Erection of Forts—Quarrels with the English—Growth of Acadia—Quarrel between La Tour and Charnisay—La Tour's Fort—Defense by Madame La Tour—Capture by Charnisay and Massacre of the Garrison—Death of Madame La Tour— Return of Charles La Tour—Death of Charnisay— Phipps' Expedition—Pirates—1671, Settlement of Minas 31-40

CHAPTER VI.

Marquette and Joliet on the Mississippi—La Salle's Explorations—His Representations to the French King—D'Iberville and Others in the South—Settlement at Biloxi—Founding of New Orleans, 1718 .. 41-43

CHAPTER VII.

1710, Final Conquest of Acadia by the English—Oath of Allegiance—Home Life of the Acadians—Their Character, Habits and Occupations—"Neutrals"— Religion 44-49

CHAPTER VIII.

Father Rasle—Character—Labors among the Indians— Erects a Church—Dictionary of the Abenaki Language—Murder of the Priest by the English— Destruction of the Church—Monument to the Memory of Father Rasle 50-52

Contents.

CHAPTER XIII.

CHAPTER XIV.

CHAPTER XV.

CHAPTER XVI.

ILLUSTRATIONS

AN HISTORICAL SKETCH OF

THE ACADIANS

Their Deportation and Wanderings

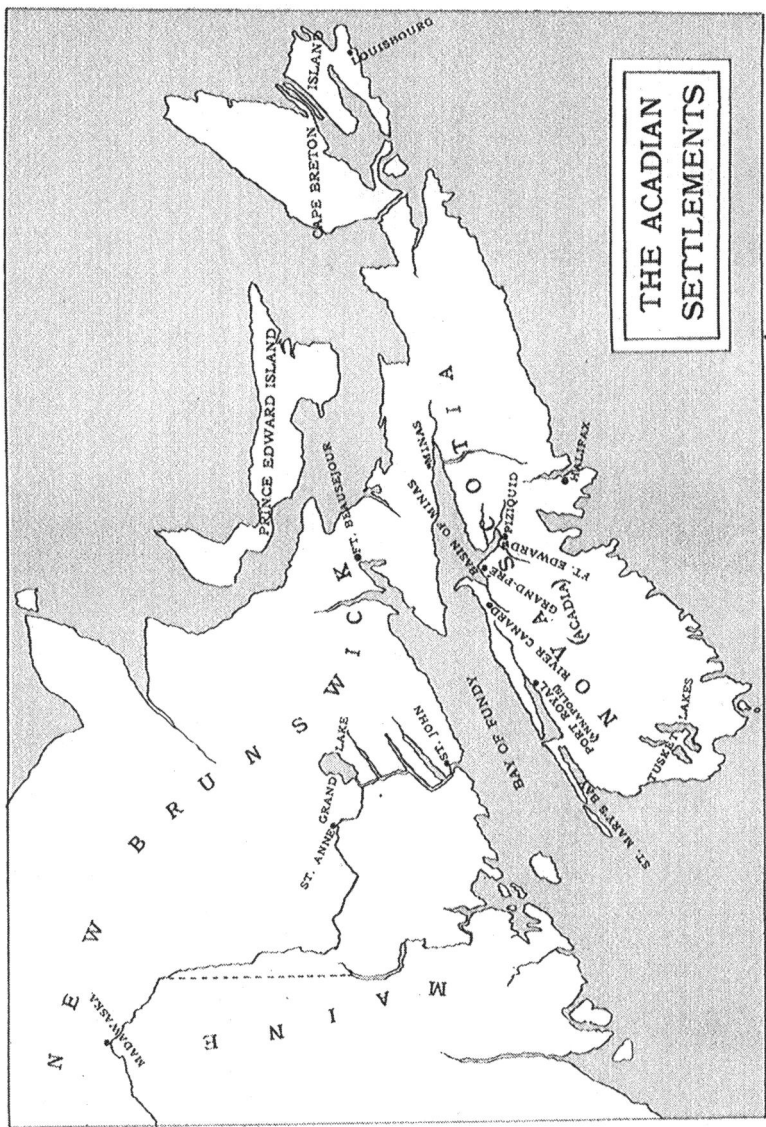

THE ACADIAN
SETTLEMENTS

LOUISBOURG

CAPE BRETON ISLAND

PRINCE EDWARD ISLAND

FT. BEAUSEJOUR

NOVA SCOTIA

MINAS

BASIN OF MINAS

PIZIQUID

HALIFAX

FT. EDWARD

GRAND-PRE

(ACADIE)

RIVER CANARD

PORT ROYAL
(ANNAPOLIS)

BAY OF FUNDY

ST. JOHN

GRAND LAKE

ST. ANNE

ST. MARY'S BAY

TUSKET LAKES

NEW BRUNSWICK

MAINE

MADAWASKA

CHAPTER I.

THE LAND OF THE ACADIANS.

*This is the forest primeval; but where are the hearts that beneath it
Leaped like the roe, when he hears in the woodland the voice of the huntsman?
Where is the thatch-roofed village, the home of Acadian farmers,—
Men whose lives glided on like rivers that water the woodlands,
Darkened by shadows of earth, but reflecting an image of heaven?
Waste are those pleasant farms, and the farmers forever departed!
Scattered like dust and leaves, when the mighty blasts of October
Seize them, and whirl them aloft, and sprinkle them far o'er the ocean.
Naught but tradition remains of the beautiful village of Grand-Pré.*

*Ye who believe in affection that hopes, and endures, and is patient,
Ye who believe in the beauty and strength of a woman's devotion,
List to the mournful tradition still sung by the pines of the forest;
List to a tale of Love in Acadie, home of the happy.*

The history of Acadia and its early settlers, the
Acadians, has a peculiar and fascinating interest for
the student of history and romance. It is a story
filled with deeds of daring and bravery, of hardships
and privations similar to those of the early pioneers
of our own colonial days, but without the reward to
their posterity which ultimately became the heritage
of the children of the English pioneers. After the
lapse of nearly a century and a half since their expulsion, when the heat of passion and the prejudice of
the earlier days have been tempered and mellowed
by time, when from the musty records of colonial
documents, and the diaries of some of the principal
actors in the great drama, historians have dug out the
facts,—we are enabled to get near in spirit to this
people, who were so little understood or appreciated
in the days of their exile and wanderings.

In order to understand the alleged necessity for,

2

but the absolute cruelty of, the expulsion of the Acadians, one must read carefully the story of the early explorations and settlements of the French and English in America; the struggle for supremacy of these two ancient enemies; their differences of character, temperament and religion; the overlapping grants of territory; the indefinite boundaries; the uncertainty which attached to rights acquired by discovery, and the claiming of vast expanses of territory, of the extent of which both the early explorer and the claimants were ignorant. It is also important to note the distinction between the Acadian and the French Canadian and the French of the State of Louisiana.

Acadia, as originally known to the French and English, embraced part of the State of Maine, all of New Brunswick, Nova Scotia, Prince Edward Island, the island of Cape Breton, and the smaller islands of the Northeast. The Acadia of the expulsion embraced the northern half of Nova Scotia, extending from the southern point northeast to and around the Basin of Minas, the southern shores of New Brunswick, and Prince Edward Island. The Acadia of " Evangeline " is found at Grand-Pré, on the basin of Minas.

The name " Acadia " is not of French origin, as many have supposed, but is a " word-ending " of the Micmac Indian language, and means " the place of," " region," " field," etc., as Shuben-acadie, Sun-acadie, and a number of others still in use in Nova Scotia.

It is found as a suffix to geographical names of Indian origin in this peninsula, while its cognate, in the Malicite Indian language of New Brunswick, is " quoddy," as Passama-quoddy, Noodi-quoddy, etc. The constant use of words with this ending by the Indians doubtless led to the adoption of the word by the first settlers for their new country. Minas, as it is now called, owes its name to the mines of copper which were discovered on the basin or bay of that name. " Les Mines " the French called the bay and surrounding country.

Minas may be understood to include all the land bordering on the basin of Minas, but more particularly on the south and west, including the rivers Gaspereau, Cornwallis, Canard, Habitant and Pereau. This will embrace the present towns and villages of Avonport, Hortonville, Grand-Pré, Gaspereau, Wolfville, Port Williams, New Minas, Kentville, Starr's Point, Canard, Cornwallis and Pereau. Piziquid, now Windsor, was also included in Minas, and for the purposes of the sketch, is still a part of Minas. These places are often referred to by their distinctive names, and again under the general term " Minas."

Acadia was settled by families, rather than by adventurers, explorers and traders, as was the case with the settlements of the St. Lawrence and lower Mississippi. If, therefore, we were to judge this people by their brethren in New Orleans, or even by those of Canada proper, we would do them injustice.

Let us consider, briefly, the first attempts at settlement in Acadia, at Port Royal, as early as 1604, and on the St. John's River, New Brunswick, about the same time; Champlain's explorations of the St. Lawrence and the Great Lakes, and the lake which bears his name; the French settlement at the South; the English colonists of New England and Virginia; the relation of the mother countries; the period of Neutrality; and the final expulsion of the Acadians from Nova Scotia in the autumn of 1755.

Annapolis (Port Royal).

CHAPTER II.

It was not until 1605 that the French succeeded in planting a permanent colony in New France. The first attempt was made at Port Royal (Annapolis) by a Huguenot nobleman—De Monts. He was given, by Henry IV, the right to plant a colony in New France, the grant including the territory as far south as the forty-sixth parallel of latitude. De Monts was made Lieutenant-General, with vice-regal powers over Nova Scotia, and given a monopoly of the fur trade.

Accompanied by Samuel Champlain and others, he sailed from Havre, in March, 1604. He touched at Havre, near Cape Sable, and later entered the bay of Fundy and discovered the beautiful sheltered harbor of Annapolis basin, but did not stop to fully explore its surroundings. He sailed to the mouth of the St. John River, and thence to the St. Croix, where he spent the first winter.

In the fall of 1605 he removed his little band to Port Royal (Annapolis), where the first real efforts to plant a colony were made. Champlain began at once to explore the coast as far south as Cape Cod, and made careful surveys and maps of the country. As early as 1603 Champlain, with Pontgravé, had entered the mouth of the St. Lawrence and ascended as far as Tadousac, near the point where the Saguenay River enters the St. Lawrence. Here they landed, but soon after proceeded up the river in a boat as far as the rapids of St. Lewis, above the place where Montreal now stands. They were greatly pleased with the country, and its prospects for trade and settlement.

Champlain returned to France in the fall, and in the following spring came over again with De Monts. He again returned to France in 1607. His explorations of the St. Lawrence had familiarized him with the country, and impressed him with the importance of establishing a trading post in that region. He suggested the matter to De Monts, who, in the following spring, upon his return, sent him and Pontgravé on an expedition for further exploration, and to establish the post. After again reaching Tadousac, they continued up the river to a place called by the Indians " Quebec," or the " Narrows." Here they concluded to form a settlement, and began at once the erection of houses, the planting of corn and grain, and the establishing and developing of the fur trade, so that, in a short time, the little colony assumed at least the air of prosperity if not the reality.

Champlain made friends with the Algonquin and Huron Indians, who were at war with the neighboring Iroquois. Ascending the Sorel River with his allies as far as the falls of Chambley, he sent his boats back with the crew, and proceeded with his

Indians in canoes up the river to the beautiful lake which bears his name. Here, near the present site of Fort Ticonderoga, they met on the lake a force of Iroquois. Both parties landed and threw up a barricade of trees and earthworks, and on the following day engaged in battle. The arquebuses or muskets of Champlain and his men were too much for the Iroquois, and an easy victory was won by Champlain and his Indian allies. The war thus begun was destined to be a costly one to the French, for the Iroquois were ever afterward their bitter enemies, and continued to harass them from time to time until English supremacy was established.

The early years of the colony were not very prosperous. This was not due to any fault of Champlain, but rather to indifference and lack of appreciation of the extent and value of the new country on the part of the home government. Champlain continued his explorations; going from the upper waters of the Ottawa, he crossed by land to Lake Huron, and explored its northern and eastern shores for some distance.

Much of the early history of this section centers around the life of Champlain, and for this reason we give considerable space to the part he played in the establishment of the colony at Quebec. He was brave and daring, more of the explorer than colonizer, yet having a keen eye for strategic positions and points of vantage for his people. He was less anxious to become governor of Canada than to continue his explorations and trading.

In 1611 Champlain returned to France,* and in 1620 was appointed Governor General of the Territory. De Monts having lost standing at the Court of France, in consequence of the death of the King, in 1610 De Soissons was appointed Lieutenant Governor, and at this time brought over a number of Recollet priests who began the conversion of the Indians.

---

*While on this visit to his native land, Champlain married Helen Boulle, a Protestant, and brought her with him to his new home. After his death she became an Ursuline nun.

CHAPTER III.

MISSIONARIES.

The Recollet and Jesuit missionaries pressed on into the vast and unknown wilderness about Lakes Superior, Huron and Michigan, and in later years traversed the streams flowing into the Mississippi, and down that river to its mouth. They established missions, and labored zealously to convert the Indians. They were the pioneers of Christian civilization in the far West. Side by side with, and often in advance of the fur trader and explorer, we find these zealous, self-sacrificing priests leading the way into the heart of the wilderness, enduring inconceivable hardships, but never despairing in the good work. They traversed the country from Nova Scotia by way of the rivers and great lakes down through the valleys of the Ohio and Mississippi, marking out and indicating to those who were to follow in less peaceful pursuits the points of importance on these rivers.

The colony at Quebec entered upon a prosperous career, and the population was largely increased by immigration from France. Champlain was in charge of the fortifications when, in 1628, an English fleet, under the command of Captain Kirk, appeared before the city and demanded its surrender. This was refused, and the English commander, after committing some depredations in the vicinity, sailed away, only to return a year later, when Champlain, on account of lack of supplies, which had been intercepted on their way to Quebec, surrendered the fort. He was made prisoner and carried to England, and was not released until the treaty of St. Germains in 1632. The prosperity of the colony depended largely on a single industry, that of trading in peltries; and in pursuit of this calling the hunters and traders braved the dangers of lurking savages, shot the rapids in their bark canoes, ventured upon the broad bosom of the stormy lakes, and patiently endured suffering from the bitter cold of the Canadian winter. The farmer was handicapped by the shortness of the summers and the severity of the winters, and by a sterile and unresponsive soil.

CHAPTER IV.

Acadia proper, so far as actual occupation and settlement were concerned, regardless of grants and
claims, comprised the present peninsula of Nova
Scotia—particularly the western part—and New
Brunswick, including the eastern part of Maine. The
little colony, numbering less than one hundred,
passed the first winter after landing at the mouth of
the St. Croix River. A winter of unusual severity,
together with the lack of proper food, and hardships
and sufferings untold, thinned their ranks to one-half
by spring. The survivors cruised along the coast as
far south as Cape Cod in search of a more suitable
place to form a settlement, but finally returned, and
entered the narrow opening, between high and per-
pendicular rocks, forming the entrance to the Annapolis Basin, now known as " Digby Gut," sailed up
the Basin to Port Royal, and made preparations to
spend the second (1605) winter.

De Monts, leaving Pontgravé in command, returned to France. C. C. Smith, in his " History of
Acadia," says: " After a winter of great suffering,
and weary with waiting for succor, Pontgravé determined to set sail for France, leaving only two men
to guard the buildings and other property. He had
just sailed when Jean de Poutrincourt, the lieutenant

of De Monts, arrived with the long-expected help. Measures were at once taken to recall Pontgravé, if he could be found on the coast, and these were fortunately successful. He was discovered at Cape Sable and at once returned, but soon after sailed for France."

The following winter, according to the report of Champlain and Lescarbot, passed very pleasantly; but in the early summer orders to abandon the settlement were received from De Monts, whose monopoly of the fur trade with the Indians had been rescinded. Many of the settlers reluctantly left their homes, and while most of them reached St. Malo in the fall of 1607, a few joined the Micmac Indians. Thus perished the first French colony of Acadia.

Three years later Poutrincourt brought over a number of families and founded a colony on the site of the abandoned settlement. The deserted houses were again occupied. Fires were lighted in the old-fashioned, rudely-constructed fireplaces, and the smoke again curled in fleecy clouds towards the heavens. The little place took on an air of activity, and a bright future seemed to be in store for the new enterprise.

The colonists were, however, doomed to bitter disappointment. The English colonists of Virginia, hearing of the attempts of the French to settle in Acadia and the north, on territory which England claimed by right of the discovery of the Cabots in 1497, but on which no attempt at settlement had as

Magazine in old Fort, Annapolis.

yet been made, at once dispatched several vessels under Captain Argall to destroy the feeble settlements. This squadron appeared off Mt. Desert Island, where a little band of priests had established themselves for the conversion of the Indians. After completely destroying all the possessions of the missionaries, and committing other outrages, Argall sailed across the Bay of Fundy to the Port Royal settlement, destroyed its buildings, killed the cattle, seized what plunder he wanted, and sailed away to Virginia, leaving the inhabitants to support themselves as best they could.

It does not appear that France ever protested against this outrage. As many of the earlier attempts at settlement were made by private individuals at their own expense, the government paid little or no attention to them, and was apparently indifferent to their fate.

A few of the colonists were taken to Virginia and sold into slavery. The colony was not abandoned; those who remained set about tilling the soil, and gathering about them the necessaries of life. The country around Annapolis, or Port Royal, as it then was called, began to be settled. It was a French settlement on territory claimed by the English, although no settlement was attempted by the latter until 1621, when Sir William Alexander, a Scotchman, obtained a grant from King James for the lordship and baronetcy of the territory of Nova Scotia and New Brunswick. Under this grant he made several attempts to colonize the country,* but without success. Four years later he attempted to infuse life into his scheme by parceling out the territory into baronetcies. This, too, failed, and the treaty of St. Germains, in 1632, gave to France all the territory occupied by the English in Nova Scotio, or Acadia, and New Brunswick.

In 1654, war having again been declared between England and France, Cromwell secretly ordered that the whole of Acadia be subjected by the English, and Captain Sedgwick and Captain John Leverett, of Boston, made the conquest. For the third time the Acadians were driven from their homes, and for ten years England ruled the colony.

---

* The small town of Granville, on the north side of the Annapolis river, opposite the present town of Annapolis, marks the site of the Scotch settlement of Sir William Alexander.

CHAPTER V.

Charles de la Tour and D'Aulnay-Charnisay were given grants of certain portions of New Brunswick, by Louis XIII, through Chevalier Razilla, who was appointed Governor of the whole of Acadia. Razilla sent them out as his lieutenants, giving to La Tour the portion east of the St. Croix River, and to Charnisay the portion west of the river. Both erected forts and began trading with the Indians.

Heretofore the English had been the aggressors in the various wars which had extended from the old world to the new, and had attacked their French neighbors on the north, meeting with but feeble resistance. The French looked with a jealous eye on the encroachments of the English colonists upon the territory ceded to France in 1632, and in a spirit of revenge for the acts of Argall, as well as to maintain the French authority over the ceded territory, the first blow was struck against the English Colonists by La Tour.

Having established himself at the mouth of the St. John River, and later at Castine, on Penobscot Bay, he, shortly after his appointment by Governor Razilla, attacked and drove away a small party of Plymouth traders and fishermen, who had set up a trading station at Machias. Charnisay treated another party of Plymouth traders in the same way. In 1633 he destroyed their fort at the mouth of the Penobscot River, but showed mercy to all the men in charge of the place, gave them their liberty, and told them to make known to their friends farther down the coast that it was his intention to disperse them the following year.

In retaliation for these attacks the Plymouth Company hired and dispatched a vessel, under Girling, and their own bark under the celebrated Miles Standish, to dispossess the French. In the attacks of Charnisay and La Tour it must be remembered that the people of Port Royal and Minas did not participate. Charnisay's fort was attacked by the English colonists; these were permitted to exhaust their ammunition, and having failed to reduce the fort they sailed away, practically defeated.

Razilla brought with him from France forty families and settled at La Havre, on the south coast of the Peninsula, near Cape Sable, and at the same point where Poutrincourt landed in 1607. He died in 1636. His possessions passed to his brother, but Charnisay, being a relative, gained control. He afterwards joined this colony to that of Port Royal, and moved his people to that point, rebuilt the fort, and sent to France for twenty additional families.

Port Royal now became the principal settlement and the capital of the province. Across the Bay of Fundy from Port Royal, at the mouth of the St. Croix, the St. John, and farther south, in the present

State of Maine, at the mouth of the Penobscot River, were French settlements. With these settlements the people of Acadia were in close touch. At the same time it is necessary to follow the growth and development of the Acadian proper, of Port Royal and the country extending northeast from that point to and including the Minas Basin region.

Here grew into being a people practically owing allegiance to no government, although nominally under the French, for many years, and then passing back and forwards, from French to English, as the fortunes of war or the caprice of European statesmen decided. Cut off from the mainland by the Bay of Fundy, and extending their settlements to the eastward, they gradually became isolated from the rest of the new world, and only came in contact with it as the marketing of their products rendered it necessary, or as the advent of a fishing or trading vessel put them in communication with the outer world. They became the farmers and herdsmen of the northeast, and supplied the garrisons and the fishing fleets of the banks of Newfoundland with their butter and eggs, their fresh meats and vegetables. Across the Bay of Fundy their fellow countrymen were not faring so well. La Tour, who held precisely the same kind of commission as Charnisay, was in charge of the fort at St. John, where the present city of that name now stands.

Charnisay established his fort at Castine, on the Penobscot Bay. The two men soon became jealous

3

of each other, and a bitter quarrel ensued. The desire on the part of each to monopolize the fur trade with the Indians, and the fact that each thought that he should be governor of this part of the Province, led to open hostilities between the two leaders. Charnisay charged La Tour with being disloyal and a traitor to France. The charge is not borne out by the facts, yet the promptness with which La Tour afterwards solicited the aid of the colonists at Boston in his behalf against Charnisay was sufficient to justify the statement at least. Claude La Tour, the father of Charles La Tour, sailed for France to obtain supplies for the fort. At the mouth of the St. Lawrence he was taken prisoner by the English under David Kirk and sent to England. He was treated with special favor by the English court and married an English lady.

Through the influence of his English wife he agreed to make an attempt to have his son surrender the fort in his charge to the English. The son was, however, loyal to France, and stood out bravely against the attacks of his father. The elder La Tour was unable to make good his promise to the English, and as a consequence they had no further use for him. He had also forfeited the confidence and respect of his own nation by his acts. Three times he had assaulted the fort and each time unsuccessfully. The English doubted the good faith of the assaults.

The old man was now reduced to poverty, but in his dire distress his English wife would not desert him. They finally joined the English colonists who had settled at Granville, on the opposite side of the bay, near the present site of Annapolis. The few settlers who remained of the band led by Sir William Alexander were still within the shadow of the fort at Annapolis. After many hardships and sufferings the elder La Tour and his wife were given shelter by the son, who erected a small lodge for them outside the walls of his fort at St. John, and provided for their wants; but there was never much social intercourse between them.

La Tour's fort was strongly built, and within the stockade were two stone houses, a magazine and stables for cattle. Twenty cannon composed its heavy armament. Here in the wilds of America lived Charles La Tour in a style and luxury rivaling that of the knights and barons of the Middle Ages. The streams, the sea and the forests furnished the choicest meats and fish for his table, while to these were added the luxuries of France, brought over in vessels trading in furs, etc.

La Tour and Charnisay each tried to enlist Massachusetts in his behalf, but to little purpose. Charnisay visited France to complain against La Tour, and if possible to have him shorn of his authority in the Colony and sent to France for punishment. By reason of his superior influence at Court at this time he was successful in securing the order, and returned to put it into execution. His rival had, in the meantime, visited Boston, and was hospitably received, but was unable to secure any direct aid from the colony other than to be permitted to hire four vessels and a pinnace to aid him in his defence.

The military forces of the rival Governors were about equal. Charnisay, with about five hundred men in armed ships, attacked Fort La Tour, but was driven away. There was a lull in the proceedings, and during the interim La Tour went to Quebec to lay the matter before the Governor of that province, and to secure his friendly offices to effect a settlement of the difficulties. He left the fort during his absence in charge of his wife. Madame La Tour was a Huguenot, endowed with courage, energy and the spirit of her ancestors. She was no more willing to surrender the fort than was her husband. In the absence of her husband Charnisay made a second attack on the fort. Madame La Tour took charge of the garrison, and from the bastions directed the cannonade on the enemy's ships. Again Charnisay was compelled to withdraw.

What valor had failed to accomplish treachery finally effected, and on his third attempt Charnisay, through the aid of a treacherous sentry, gained admission to the fort. Seeing herself betrayed, the lady rose to the occasion, and, aided by the loyal men of the garrison, fought with the valor of a knight of old. " Fight, men, for our honor and the fort! " she cried. The fight was fierce; many were killed on both sides. Charnisay proposed that the garrison capitulate, promising life and liberty to all. The terms were accepted by Madame La Tour, but Charnisay afterwards violated his promise, and Madame La Tour was compelled to witness, with a rope around her own neck, the execution of every member of the garrison, eighteen in all. She was told that she was to be the last to suffer. Her life was spared, but the atrocities she was compelled to witness, the loss of the fort, the absence of her husband, and the terrible strain she had been under for so long, broke her health, and she died a few days afterwards. Charnisay secured booty to the value of ten thousand pounds. He had now the whole of Acadia to himself, and began to erect mills and build ships. For a short time the colony was prosperous. He received honors from France, and in 1647 was commissioned Governor, but his reign was of short duration.

La Tour, upon his return from Quebec, was crushed and heartbroken over the death of his wife and the devastation wrought by his enemy. Two years later he sailed for France, and laid the facts of Charnisay's tyranny so effectively before the Court, that he not only secured a restoration of his title and privileges, but was made Charnisay's successor. After two years spent in France he returned as Governor and Lieutenant General of Acadia, determined to retrieve his fortunes and avenge the death of his wife. In the interim Charnisay was drowned, and upon the arrival of La Tour the widow of Charnisay prepared to defend the rights of herself and her children against the enemy of her husband. The matters

in dispute were amicably arranged by the marriage of
La Tour to the widow of Charnisay. The honeymoon
was interrupted by a detachment of English soldiers,
under the command of Captain Robert Sedgwick,
who forced the fort to surrender, largely on account
of the lack of provisions. La Tour obtained from
Cromwell a large grant of land for himself and two
Englishmen, but becoming pecuniarily embarrassed
he sold his interests to his partners. Thus ended the
struggles between Charnisay and La Tour, one of the
romances of the early days of Acadia.

From 1656 until 1668 Acadia was under the control of the English, when it was ceded to France with
" undefined limits," a phrase fruitful of much trouble. From 1668 until 1713, when Acadia passed
finally into the possession of the English, it changed
no less than ten times from one power to the other.
By the treaty of Utrecht it was finally relinquished
to the English.

In 1690, hostilities being again renewed between
the mother countries, an expedition was fitted out at
Boston under the supervision of Sir William Phipps,
and sent to destroy the settlements at Port Royal and
St. John. With a frigate of forty guns, two sloops
with twenty-four guns, five smaller vessels, and transports for seven hnudred men, he reduced St. John
and Port Royal, and secured booty enough to pay the
entire expense of the expedition. Phipps was appointed Governor of Massachusetts, which nominally
included Acadia.

Ruins of French Fort, Annapolis.

The treaty of Ryswick seven years later gave the country back to France. With each transfer of the Acadians they were plundered by their English neighbors; they were so much easier to reach than the French Canadian.

France, after the treaty of Ryswick, sent Villebon in the ship Union with supplies and recruits for the garrison, and presents for the Indians. On his arrival at Port Royal he was told of the hardships the people had recently suffered, and that the English were probably yet in the waters of the Bay of Fundy. After consultation Villebon decided to leave the Union at Port Royal, cross the bay and occupy Fort Jemseg on the St. John River.

Scarcely had he reached St. John before there arrived in the harbor of Port Royal two ships manned by English and colonial pirates. They landed and pillaged the remains of the place, burned twelve houses, crossed the Annapolis River to Granville, burned sixteen houses, killed the cattle, hanged some of the inhabitants, burned others, seized all the plunder, including the entire cargo of the Union, and sailed away.

Between 1604, the date of De Monts' arrival in Acadia, and 1667, when the treaty of Breda, by which England surrendered Acadia to France, was signed, a period of nearly three-quarters of a century, the population had grown but slowly. This was mainly owing to the almost constant war between the two nations, and to the jealousies and the occasional warfare between the rival claimants to various sections of the country. At the latter date probably less than five hundred whites of both nations lived in Acadia. While the settlers at Port Royal were gradually pushing up the river, it was not until 1671 that a settlement was affected at Minas, although the region had been known for many years. About this time Pierre Theriot, Antoine Landry, Claud Landry and Rene La Blanc began a settlement at Minas. From this time on the northeastern section of the peninsula began to develop. New settlers came each year, and, being isolated from the rest of the world, they were permitted to grow and flourish (with occasional interruptions and exactions on the part of both England and France) for nearly a hundred years.

CHAPTER VI.

As early as 1673, Marquette, a Jesuit missionary, and Joliet, a fur trader, floated down the Wisconsin into the Mississippi River, and down that stream as far as the mouth of the Arkansas. Here they stopped with some friendly Indians, who warned them against the hostile tribes farther down the river.

They returned to the north again, satisfied that they had reached a point not far from the mouth of the great river. It remained for La Salle, who had established a trading post on Lake Ontario, and who had previously discovered the Ohio and other rivers flowing into the Mississippi, to successfully explore it to its mouth, as well as northward to the falls of St. Anthony. In 1682 he floated down the stream to the Gulf. He saw and appreciated the great advantage of establishing a colony near its mouth, in order to control the two great water routes to the interior, the St. Lawrence being already in the possession of the French. He returned to France and placed the matter before the King, with all the fervor and zeal of his nature. His Majesty listened to the glowing description, but not appreciating the importance of so rich a discovery, did not become enthusiastic over the project. It was only through the combined efforts of La Salle, Remonville, D'Iberville, and his brother Bienville, that the King finally became convinced of the importance of undertaking the enterprise.

Several expeditions were soon thereafter fitted out, one under the direction of La Salle, and one under D'Iberville and his brother, Bienville. The captain of La Salle's expedition, failing to find the mouth of the river, sailed farther south, and landed in Texas. Here the colony was left, while La Salle started on foot for Canada to seek aid for the suffering settlers. Some of his party mutinied, and after a few days' journey, La Salle was secretly murdered. The Spaniards, upon whose territory the expedition had landed, shortly afterward destroyed the colonists, or carried into slavery those they did not put to death.

D'Iberville and his brother formed a settlement at Biloxi, at the head of Biloxi Bay, east of the Mississippi River. D'Iberville was governor of the colony at first, but in 1704 Bienville succeeded to the direction of affairs. A settlement was formed at Mobile, and one on the lower Mississippi, about fifty miles from its mouth. In 1710 the colony was reduced to famine. Bienville was accused of mismanagement. A new Governor was appointed, who brought with him a commission for Bienville as Lieutenant Governor. The latter, having shortly afterward quarreled with his superior, was sent by the Governor on an expedition up the river, in the hope that the Indians would kill him. He ascended to Natchez, where he made friends with the Indians and established a small trading station. In 1718 he founded New Orleans, and was made Governor of the Province. The seat of government was transferred from Mobile to New Orleans.

France saw the rapid encroachment of the English and Spanish, realized the necessity of holding the advantage she had gained in this territory, and at once began to rush in new immigrants without regard to their character. All grades of French life, from the highest to the lowest, were dumped promiscuously into the settlement.

The weakness of the French colonies was due in part to the lack of support by the home government, and to the smallness of their numbers, but chiefly to the fact that their settlements were mostly trading devices. Their neighbors, the English, and even the Spaniards, sought to establish homes for themselves.

We now find the French with the above-mentioned settlements at the south, one of considerable strength at Quebec, one at Port Royal and one at Louisbourg on Cape Breton Island. Already they had begun to establish a chain of forts extending from the St. Lawrence by way of the great lakes, the Alleghenies, the Ohio and the Mississippi Rivers to New Orleans. Many of these forts figured prominently in the wars which followed in the next fifty years.

CHAPTER VII.

In September, 1710, when the harvests were gathered, the fall crops planted, and preparations being made for the coming winter, the inhabitants of Port Royal were greatly surprised to see a most formidable fleet coming up the basin to attack Port Royal. The fort commands a view of the inland bay for a long distance. Four regiments of New England troops landed without resistance. On the first of October three batteries were opened within two hundred yards of the fort, and after a bombardment of twenty-four hours it capitulated. By the terms of surrender the soldiers were to be transported to France, and the French inhabitants living within cannon-shot of Port Royal were to be protected in person and property for two years, on taking the oath of allegiance to the Queen of England; or they were to be allowed to move to Canada or Newfoundland. Port Royal became Annapolis, and Acadia forever ceased to be a Province of France. By the treaty of Utrecht (1713) Acadia passed to Great Britain, but France was left in undisputed possession of Cape Breton Island.

The French Government, in order to check the English in Nova Scotia, began the fortification of Louisbourg, and invited the Acadians to its protection. The English, fearing this concentration of

Old Church at Grand-Pré, built 1804.

strength at Louisbourg, forbade the movement, and tacitly allowed them to stay in their accustomed places, from time to time demanding of them that they take the oath of allegiance. This the Acadians were willing to do if they might be exempted from bearing arms against their brothers in Canada, Cape Breton and the mother country. In other words, as to England's ancient enemy they wished to remain neutral.

Now begins their distinct existence under English rule as "neutrals." For almost thirty years they enjoyed comparative peace. They tilled their land, planted fruit trees and raised stock. The meadow lands were reclaimed from the sea by the erection of dykes, and thus afforded most excellent pasturage for their cattle. The mechanic and artisan, the blacksmith, the carpenter, the wagonmaker and the cobbler each found a demand for his services. Fishing formed a very important industry, and many were engaged in this occupation, while not a few continued to deal in peltries with the neighboring tribes of Indians, particularly the Micmacs. A few colonists from Massachusetts settled among them, which was a little leaven inspiring them to put forth every effort to improve their condition.

The English soldiery were haughty and discourteous, and heaped much abuse and many indignities upon the neutrals. These, however, peaceably endured, still cherishing the hope that they might again become the subjects of France. They were a highly moral, religious and kind-hearted people. The Acadian was not inclined to leave his native village, or to break away from the traditions of his ancestors. Cheerful in spirit, easily satisfied as to his necessities, content with little, he naturally was not disposed to contend for his rights. Palfrey says: " There appears to be no doubt that they were a virtuous, simpleminded, industrious, unambitious, religious people." English and American writers have shown that they were not the dangerous and warlike people they have sometimes been painted by the prejudiced writers of colonial days.

We may naturally infer that they were neither saints nor demons, but a fair sample of the French peasant born on American soil and endeavoring to improve his condition in life under very trying circumstances.

" Thus, at peace with God and the world, the farmer of Grand-Pré

Lived on his sunny farm, and Evangeline governed his household.

Many a youth, as he knelt in the church and opened his missal,

Fixed his eyes upon her as the saint of his deepest devotion;

Happy was he who might touch her hand or the hem of her garment!

Many a suitor came to her door, by the darkness befriended,

And, as he knocked and waited to hear the sound of her footsteps,

Knew not which beat the louder, his heart or the knocker of iron;

Or at the joyous feast of the Patron Saint of the village,

Bolder grew, and pressed her hand in the dance as he whispered

Hurried words of love, that seemed a part of the music.
But, among all who came, young Gabriel only was welcome;
Gabriel Lajeunesse, the son of Basil the blacksmith."

C. C. Smith says that our poet Longfellow, in " Evangeline," " throws a somewhat false and distorted light over the character of the Acadians." " They were not the peaceable and happy people they are commonly supposed to have been; and their houses were by no means the vine-clad, picturesque and strongly-built houses or cottages described by the poet. The people were notably quarrelsome among themselves, and to the last degree superstitious." This statement is not borne out by the facts. It may be true, and was no doubt the case at certain periods of their existence, that their houses were not strongly built, or vine-clad, for when we recall the fact that their dwellings were destroyed no less than ten or twelve times, it is not at all likely that strongly-built houses should each time take the place of those destroyed.

We have it on good authority, however, that many substantial houses were erected, among them stone buildings of one and two stories, and not a few quite pretentious structures were reared by the wealthier class, both at Minas and Port Royal. Longfellow's inquiry, " Where is the thatched-roofed village, the home of the Acadian farmer?" does not throw a distorted light on the home of the Acadian farmer. The æsthetic tastes of their French ancestors were not wanting in these descendants born in the new world, and flowers adorned their yards and humble homes in great profusion, while the tall and graceful Normandy poplar and willow to-day mark the site of many a ruined Acadian home. It is altogether likely that the home of the Acadian would compare favorably at all times with that of his New England neighbor under like conditions.

Their home life was similar to that of the peasants from whom they were descended, with greater freedom of action, when not harassed by a brutal soldiery or by the pirates who infested the coast. The men and boys built dykes to " shut out the turbulent tides," and reclaimed vast stretches of rich meadow land; they tilled the soil and gathered the harvests; wood was cut for the winter, and logs for the old-fashioned " up-and-down saw of a single stroke." The carpenter and blacksmith, the mason, the cobbler and the miller each in his way contributed to the wealth of the colony. The maiden, gowned in her modest home-spun garments, assisted her mother in the household duties, sewing, knitting, baking, scrubbing, spinning, weaving, and performing a hundred other tasks that fall to the lot of women. In turn she was shepherdess and milk-maid, and in summer she " raked the meadows sweet with hay," but no proud judge ever rode by to disturb the maiden's serenity. In the " hay-making " she was assisted by the strong-limbed and light-hearted lads of her village, and many a friendly contest was entered into by the young men in pitching hay, that the victor

Old Poplar Trees, Grand-Pré.

might win the approving smile or nod of the queen of the hay field. The old dinner bell that hung in the forks of the tree, or swung between two upright posts, pealed forth its welcome notes, calling the toiler from hay-field or from harvest-field to a bountiful repast of fish, game and wild fruits.

There was another bell, with a silvery tone, which swung high in the tower of the church, that morning, noon and night called the faithful to prayer, as does the muezzin the Moslem. Down on his knees went the simple son of Acadia, and thus kneeling he offered up a fervent prayer to the Master or an *Ave Maria* to the Virgin. On Sunday the villagers and the country people were early astir, and old and young alike attended church, lingering after the services to discuss crops and local affairs, or to inquire after the health of the absent ones.

The Acadian has been charged with being superstitious and ignorant. Doubtless he was both,—it was a superstitious age; and while his New England neighbor, provided with schools, churches and an educated ministry, was busy burning witches and cropping the ears of Quakers, it is not to be expected that the Acadian would be entirely devoid of some of the weaknesses which marred the character of the early Puritans of New England. With all his virtues —and they were many—the Puritan had no equal for superstition, bigotry and cruelty among the colonists of North America. In all Acadian history we can find no parallel for Salem and its witch-burning.

4

CHAPTER VIII.

Sebastian Rasle, often improperly spelled Raale, or Rale, was born at Dole, France, of distinguished family. He was highly educated, and at one time taught Greek in the Jesuit college of Nimes. At his own request he was appointed to the missions in Canada, and for a while was stationed at Quebec. In 1695 he was placed in charge of the station at Norridgewock, on the Kennebec River. Here he began his work among the Indians, and made a very thorough study of the Abenaki language. By sharing the dangers and hardships of the tribe he soon became a power among them. The French authorities at Quebec attempted to use this influence against the English, and entered into correspondence with Rasle. It has been stated that Rasle instigated the attacks of the Indians on the English settlements along the coast. He really, however, only tried to prevent the Abenaki from having any dealings with the English, or becoming imbued with the Protestant faith.

Public opinion in Boston and New England became aroused against the priest, and as early as 1705 the Council of Boston put a price on his head. Captain Hilton, at the head of two hundred and seventy men, including forty-five New Englanders, attempted his capture. Norridgewock was surprised and its church burned, but Father Rasle escaped to the woods with his papers. When peace was declared in 1715, he, with the aid of the French Governor, began the erection of a new church at the same place, which when completed " would excite admiration in Europe." It was supplied with all the beautiful and costly vestments and symbols of Roman Catholic worship, and services were conducted with great dignity and pomp—forty Indian boys acting as acolytes. The Massachusetts authorities engaged in a correspondence with Father Rasle, with a view of decoying him to Boston; failing in this, they sent parties to seize him.

In January, 1725, Colonel Westbrook, with three hundred men, reached the mission, burned the magnificent church, and pillaged Father Rasle's home, but failed to capture him. They found an iron box, which contained, besides his papers and his correspondence with the authorities at Quebec, a dictionary of the Abenaki language, the work of the priest, and which is to-day preserved in the library of Harvard College. A year later another body of one hundred and eight men from Fort Richmond, at dead of night, when all the inmates were peaceably sleeping, stole in upon the little station of Norridgewock, seized Father Rasle and put him to death, it is said at the foot of the mission cross. Many Indians were killed in this night attack, among whom were seven chiefs who attempted to save the life of their beloved priest. The priest's body was mutilated and left without burial. A few days later the Indians returned and buried the remains.

The French authorities vainly demanded reparation for this outrage. One hundred and nine years after the murder of Father Rasle a monument was erected and dedicated to his memory, Bishop Fenwick, of Boston,—(that city which sought so long to, and eventually did, accomplish the missionary's death),—officiating at the dedication.

The estimates of the character of Father Rasle are as various as the Roman Catholic and Protestant writers could make them, one calling him "an infamous villain," the other "a saint and hero." He died in the performance of his duties, and the Catholic estimate of his character is doubtless the nearer correct.

CHAPTER IX.

PREPARATIONS FOR THE FINAL STRUGGLE.

During the thirty years of peace the only events of any consequence which occurred to disturb the general tranquillity were the attack on the English by the Abenaki Indians, and the murder of Father Rasle. From this time until the breaking out of hostilities between France and England, in 1745, the French dream of a great Empire west of the mountains and along the interior water-routes, with the control of the two great natural outlets, the St. Lawrence and Mississippi Rivers, had not been despaired of. Active preparations were being made to strengthen their position from one river to the other, by way of the great lakes; and to this end more than sixty forts were erected. The first and strongest of these was the series of fortifications at Louisbourg, on Cape Breton Island, which was called the Gibraltar of America. The French spent over five million pounds on these works, and believed them to be impregnable. Louisbourg commanded the entrance to the St. Lawrence through its deepest channel.

For a quarter of a century France had devoted her energies to the completion of this stronghold, and now its somber walls and towers stood like frowning giants above the northern seas as a menace to their ancient enemy. The town was nearly three miles in

circumference, and was surrounded by a rampart of
stone from thirty to thirty-six feet high, and a ditch
or moat in front eighty feet wide. There were six
bastions and eight batteries, containing embrasures
for one hundred cannon and eight mortars. In addition there were at the entrance to the harbor two
batteries, one of which was on a high hill overlooking
the entrance and in a very commanding position.
The Citadel was in the gorge of the King's bastion.
The stately stone Church, Nunnery and Hospital
were in the center of the town. All the streets
crossed at right angles, and communication was had
with the harbor by means of five gates in the wall on
that side of the town. The houses were constructed
for the most part of stone, and the town had the appearance of being unusually ancient and substantial
for so new a country.

The fort at Crown Point, on Lake Champlain,
guarded the entrance into Canada from the Hudson
Valley. Quebec was strengthened. Other fortifications of considerable strength and importance were
Niagara, Detroit, Toledo, Fort LeBœuf (Waterford,
Erie County, Pa.), Presque Isle (Erie, Pa.), Fort
Venango (Franklin, Pa.), Fort Duquesne (Pitts-
burg, Pa.), and a number of others between Duquesne and New Orleans. The skill and foresight
with which these points were selected is shown by
the fact that many of them are now marked by large
and flourishing cities.

During this period the French population had not

increased with anything like the rapidity of the English. While they had military posts in abundance, they had few actual settlements, and fewer tillers of the soil. On the other hand, the English were making great progress, and increasing rapidly in population. After one hundred and fifty years of occupation the French numbered 125,000, while the English numbered 1,250,000. The third inter-colonial war, known as King George's War, was devoid of any incident of importance except the capture of Louisbourg. This strongly-fortified place yielded after a siege of six weeks by four thousand New England troops and four English war vessels, June 17th, 1745. There was nothing very brilliant or scientific about the siege, but by its successful issue the colonial troops were given confidence in their own ability, bravery and skill as soldiers, which thirty years later ranked them among the best fighting material of the world.

The capture of this stronghold by the colonial forces astonished all Europe, and Mr. Pepperell, the merchant who led the expedition, was made a baronet by the King. The next year France sent a fleet to recapture Louisbourg, but storms and disease caused them to abandon the attempt. Upon peace being again restored between France and England, the Americans were chagrined and bitterly disappointed to find that Louisbourg had been restored to France, and they had been deprived of the fruits of their victory. It is said that the drums which beat the American triumphal march into the city of Louisbourg, June 17th, 1745, thirty years after at Bunker Hill, June 17th, 1775, animated the patriots in the first fight in which the American militia ever measured swords with English veterans. This war taught the colonists that they must be prepared to defend their own interests, since England was evidently liable at any time to sacrifice colonial to her own domestic interests.

Gaspereau Valley and Village.

CHAPTER X.

In the Acadian land, on the shores of the Basin of Minas,
Distant, secluded, still, the little village of Grand-Pré
Lay in the fruitful valley. Vast meadows stretched to the eastward,
Giving the village its name, and pasture to flocks without number.
Dikes, that the hands of the farmers had raised with labor incessant,
Shut out the turbulent tides; but at stated seasons the flood-gates
Opened, and welcomed the sea to wander at will o'er the meadows.
West and south there were fields of flax, and orchards and corn-fields
Spreading afar and unfenced o'er the plain; and away to the northward
Blomidon rose, and the forests old, and aloft on the mountains
Sea-fogs pitched their tents, and mists from the mighty Atlantic
Looked on the happy valley, but ne'er from their station descended.
There, in the midst of its farms, reposed the Acadian village.

The reader naturally reverts to Port Royal and the events transpiring there. The treaty of Utrecht, which gave Louisbourg to the French, reserved all of Acadia, with that exception, to England, and gave to the Acadians one year in which to remove themselves and their movable property wherever they might desire. Those who remained could do so as subjects of Great Britain, and should enjoy the free exercise of their religion as far as the laws of the country allowed. They had also the privilege of selling their land if they desired to remove from the country. Treaties between nations at war with each other, when made with reference to the disposal of territory, are formulated without consulting the inhabitants of the country disposed of; it was so in the case of the Acadians. By reference to the outline map the reader will notice the location of Louisbourg, Fort Beausejour, Fort Edward, Halifax and

Port Royal. These were the fortified places in Nova Scotia and Cape Breton Island. Louisbourg and Fort Beausejour were occupied by the French, while over Port Royal (Annapolis) and Halifax floated the flag of England.

The land of Acadia, as known in song and story, extended from Annapolis northeast to and around Minas Basin, embracing the present counties of Annapolis and Kings, with settlements along the Canard, Piziquid, Avon and Gaspereau Rivers. This is the " Land of Evangeline." Here the simple Acadian peasant tried to live the life of a neutral between two nations contending for a continent, from one of which he was descended, whose mother tongue was his, and whose religion and traditions were in constant and irreconcilable conflict with the other. Yet the Acadian, such was his Quaker-like disposition, would have avoided, for himself and his children, all connection with the warring nations.

Here, too, occurred the last sad scene in the drama of Acadian life,—their expulsion, and the destruction of their homes. The " Neutrals," as the colonists called them, were between the upper and the nether mill-stone. On the one hand the French, at Beausejour and Louisbourg, were urging them to join their fellow countrymen against the English, and demanding of them cattle and other necessaries of life for the garrisons, threatening vengeance and the excommunication of the Church if these were refused. On the other hand, the English, whose subjects they were, forbade their trading with the French, or shipping any cattle or produce out of the country, and demanded of them all necessary supplies for the garrisons at Halifax, Annapolis and Fort Edward. Halifax was in 1749 made the seat of government.

There has been so much controversy as to the neutrality, not to say loyalty, of the Acadian, that we deem it wise at this time to investigate the matter in the light thrown about it by ancient documents and records on both sides of the controversy. He was as loyal to his English king as a man who takes an oath to support and defend his Majesty's government against all his enemies, except his greatest, can be. He took this modified oath, hoping that he might never be called upon to fight against his own people, and indeed hoping that he might not be called upon to fight at all. He was loyal, in that, with a few exceptions, he never gave aid or comfort to his Majesty's enemies. In fact, he wished to be left alone. War might be waged all around him, and he was indifferent if he were not forced to engage in it, or if he were not molested by the active participants in the struggle. He could see no reason for war, much less that he should take part in it.

It is true that he hoped that he might again be a subject of France; not that his people had ever been benefited by the acts of the French government, or its officers and agents, but because of a common religion, language and tradition.

The Acadians, from the treaty of Ryswick until the time of their dispersion, were looked upon with suspicion both by the colonists of New England and their fellow countrymen of Canada, and by the French soldiery at Louisbourg and Beausejour. If France won in the struggle for supremacy on the American continent, she would have to win without the aid of the Acadians, whom she considered her subjects, and whose aid she was constantly seeking, only to be persistently refused. What would have been their position had they aided their countrymen after having taken the oath of allegiance to England? That question has been answered by their fate, for whether they had violated their oaths or not the result would evidently have been the same. Both governments were exacting of them the things which put them in a doubtful light.

Captain Du Vivier, under orders from the French Commandant at Louisbourg, directs that " the inhabitants of Minas are ordered to acknowledge the obedience they owe to the King of France, and in consequence are called upon for the following supplies: the parish of Grand-Pré, eight horses and two men to drive them; that of the River Canard, eight horses and two men to drive them; that of Piziquid, twelve horses and three men to drive them; as also the powder horns possessed by the said inhabitants, one only being reserved for each house. The whole of the above must be brought to me on Saturday morning at 10 o'clock, at the flag which I have hoisted, and under which the deputies from the said parishes shall be assembled to pledge fidelity for themselves and for all the inhabitants of the neighborhood who shall not be called away from the labors of the harvest. All those for whom the pledge of fidelity shall be given will be held fully responsible for said pledge, and those who contravene the present order, shall be punished as rebellious subjects, and delivered into the hands of savages as enemies of the State, as we cannot refuse the demands which the savages make for all those who will not submit themselves. We enjoin upon the inhabitants who have acknowledged their submission to the King of France to acquaint us promptly with the names of all those who wish to screen themselves from the said obedience, in order that faithful subjects shall not suffer from any incursions which the savages may make."

This threat of the French Commandant to turn loose the Indians was one of the reasons urged by the Acadians for not taking the oath of allegiance to the English King. This note also contained a demand for large quantities of meat and grain. The Acadians replied as follows:

" To M. DE GANNE:

" We, the undersigned, humbly representing the inhabitants of Minas, River Canard, Piziquid, and the surrounding rivers, beg that you will be pleased to consider, that while there would be no difficulty, by virtue of the strong force which you command, in supplying yourself with the quantity of grain and meat you and Du Vivier have ordered, it would be quite impossible for us to furnish the quantity you demand, or even a smaller (since the harvest has not been so good as we hoped it would be), without placing ourselves in great peril. We hope, gentlemen, that you will not plunge us and our families into a state of total loss; and that this consideration will cause you to withdraw your savages and troops from our districts. We live under a mild and tranquil government, and we have all good reason to be faithful to it.

"Your very obedient servants,

JACQUES LE BLANC AND OTHERS.

"Minas, Octobre 13, 1744."

Under the same date the English Governor, Mascarene, writes to the deputies a very highly commendatory note, in which he says of the people of Minas and vicinity, " They are to be commended for remaining true to the allegiange which they owe to the King of Great Britain, their legitimate sovereign, notwithstanding the efforts which have been made to cause them to disregard it."

A few of the Acadians living at Chignecto, near Fort Beausejour, did leave their homes and joined the French. Governor Mascarene sent them a message to the effect that if they wished to avoid the danger which threatened them, they should do as the others had done, and give an account of their conduct and show their allegiance to the government of the King of Great Britain. " In that case you shall still have me as your friend and servant." The few who violated their oath of allegiance to the English King did so largely through the influence of the priest La Loutre. They were anxious afterward to return, and were permitted to do so by the English Government.

Haliburton, whose sympathies were naturally with the English, referring to the readiness with which the Acadians complied with the order to surrender their arms and boats, says: " The orders against the French population, directing them to surrender their arms and the giving up of their boats, were complied with in a manner which might have convinced the Government that they had no serious intention of an insurrection." The same author remarks that the Government did not always conciliate, or show a disposition to win the affections of the people. He cites the act of Captain Murray in demanding of the inhabitants of Piziquid that they furnish his detachment with wood for fuel, or he would use their houses for that purpose, and if they did not furnish timber for the repairs of the fort they would suffer military execution.

We have endeavored to give, as a fitting setting to the final scene in the tragedy of the Acadians, the early French explorations; their fruitless attempts at settlement on the eastern coast; their settlements at the mouth of the Mississippi and the character of the settlers there; the wars between the New England colonies and the Indians; the quarrels of La Tour and Charnisay; the frequent shifting of government from one power to the other; the attacks on the Acadians and the destruction of their homes. All this brings us to the period immediately preceding the final edict for their expulsion.

CHAPTER XI.

One event which occurred in the winter of 1747-8 should be mentioned at this time, since it has been unjustly charged to the inhabitants of Minas and the surrounding settlements. This was the attack of Captain Coulon de Villiers on the English garrison at Minas. It will be remembered that after the fall of Louisbourg the French sent an armament for its recapture. This attempt failed, as we have seen, and a detachment of the fleet, under Captain Ramesay, took charge of the French fort at Beausejour, at the head of a narrow neck of land which connects the peninsula of Nova Scotia with New Brunswick.

Their presence here, and the threats made against the Acadians if they did not join them in operations against the weak English garrison at Annapolis, greatly alarmed the Acadians, who feared not only the savages whom the French soldiery always had in their employ, but the New England colonists, and the authorities at Annapolis. Mascarene, the Governor of the Province of Nova Scotia, asked for reinforcements, and Governor Shirley sent five hundred troops, under Colonel Arthur Noble. Noble landed at Annapolis, and with about one hundred men started to march overland to Minas. The others started by water, but the winds and the floating ice made the passage difficult if not impossible. They were forced to land at French Cross, or Morden, more than forty miles from Grand-Pré, or Minas. Here began a weary march overland, through deep snow, in the face of severe storms, and through a trackless wilderness, over the rugged North Mountain.

After eight days of intense suffering they arrived at Grand-Pré. Here they were received with great hospitality by the people, who willingly gave up their homes for the accommodation of the soldiers. The ships with the stores reached their destination. The soldiers were quartered in twenty-four houses in the village, for a mile and a half along the highway.

It was now December, and winter had set in with all its fury. The snow was three feet deep, and the rivers and bay were full of floating ice. Noble and his soldiers were living on the best the land afforded, and were resting in apparent security. He had selected for his headquarters a stone house in the center of the village. " It was his intention to march against the French quartered at Beausejour, then under the command of Ramesay, but the severity of the winter and the depth of the snow made the venture seem impossible, so he rested content and in fancied security from attack. He was repeatedly warned against an attack by the French and Indians, the latter being much incensed against the Acadians and English, but friendly with the Canadians and French. He was told by the Acadians that it was the

5

intention of Ramesay to attack him, but he paid little heed to this warning.

Let us glance for a few moments at what was transpiring among the French. We quote from the forcible and accurate description of the only living descendant of the Acadian exiles now residing in or near Grand-Pré, Mr. John Frederick Herbin, of Wolfville, who has spent years in studying the life and character of his " mother's people."

" Meanwhile word had reached Ramesay of the arrival of the troops at Grand-Pré, and he learned that it was Colonel Noble's intention to march against him in the spring. But he was misinformed as to the number of soldiers under Noble. He was told that there were two hundred and twenty, which was less than half the actual number. Ramesay had already made two arduous but fruitless marches to Annapolis. On the return from the last of these he had severely hurt his knee, and was unable to march. Calling a council of his officers, he proposed a bold enterprise, to which they gave eager assent.

" The proposal was to attack the enemy by a rapid march and night attack on Grand-Pré. As Ramesay was unable to lead the party, the command fell to the gallant Captain Coulon De Villiers. Immediate preparations were made for the march. Provisions were collected, snow shoes and sledges were prepared, and in a short time the party was ready for the start. There was but one way to reach Grand-Pré, and that was by making the distance through the woods and

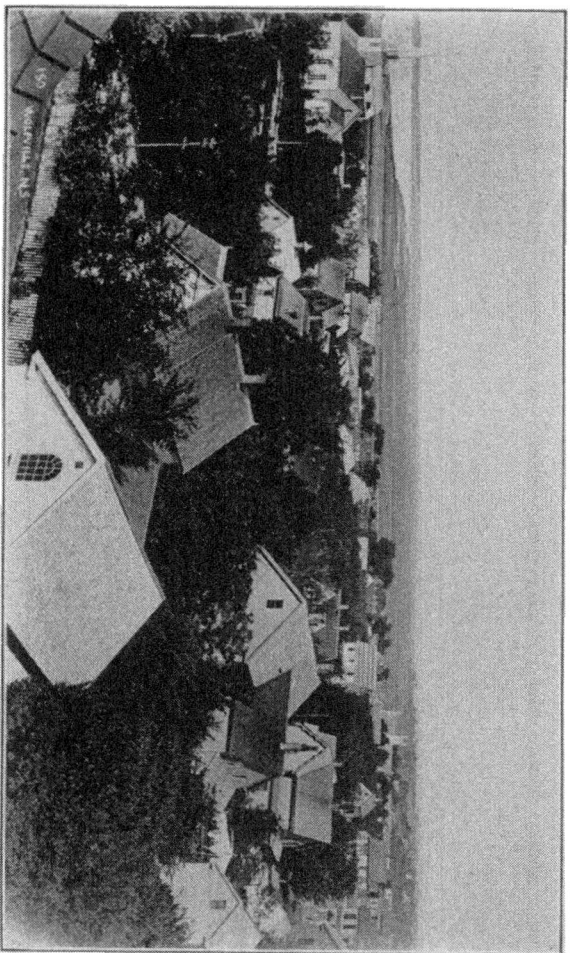

Wolfville (Grand-Pré in distance to right).

across the rivers near their head. The snow was over three feet deep, and the long march would afford but little shelter to these hardy warriors. In four days all arrangements were complete. Coulon had under his command two hundred and forty Canadians and twenty Indians. Here were the flower of the warlike Canadian *noblesse*—Coulon De Villiers, who, seven years later, defeated Washington; Beaujeau, the hero of future fights, a bold and determined warrior, without the appearance of it; the Chevalier de la Corne, Saint Pierre, Lanaudière, Saint-ours, Desligneris, Courtemanche, Repentigney, Boisherbert, Gaspé, Colombier, Marin, Lusignan.

" On the twenty-first of January the company started on its long march. Mile after mile they dragged their snow sledges along, each with its provisions. There could be wavering now. Their long, winding track was as the trail of a serpent, whose instinct led it to its prey. Over hills and through valleys and swamps they moved, till night overtook and compelled them to rest, and slumber came to their weary bodies.

" Through the storms of snow and wind, or in the sharp frost of the Acadian forests, they marched in the day time. At night they were often glad to rest in holes scooped out of the soft snow, in such shelter as the forests offered. Many a meal they ate, thawing the frozen food in their mouths. Over the mountains and gorges of the Cobequids they tramped. At the head of the bay they were met by messengers who brought them intelligence as to the exact number of the English at Grand-Pré, and what had been done there. This was startling news, but it did not deter them. They were able to procure provisions at the villages they were now passing through, and recruits were added to their ranks. On reaching the River Shubenacadie, near the head of the basin of Minas, they found it impassable from floating ice. Coulon resolved that the river must be crossed by a small party at this point to guard the road to Grand-Pré, so that intelligence might not be carried to the English of their approach. They were in territory now where the French were more favorable to the English."

It may be well to explain here that many of the settlers near the French fort on the north, and those living beyond the Basin of Minas, were influenced by their close proximity as well as their natural feelings, to say nothing of the fear of a rude soldiery, and this induced some of them to take sides with the French, while possibly some were forced to join Coulon's expedition.

These, however, must not be confused with the Acadians of Grand-Pré and the surrounding country, nor can the Acadian proper be held responsible for the acts of his brothers east of the Basin of Minas. The main body, under Coulon, continued up the river for three days before they could cross. They joined the others, and in a few days reached the town of Piziquid (Windsor), fifteen miles from Grand-Pré.

Here they rested until noon of the 10th, when they began their march through a snowstorm, moving slowly until they reached the Gaspereau River, just south of the present village of Grand-Pré, a mile and a half from their destination. Half frozen in the storm, they had to wait an hour for nightfall before they went any farther. When it grew dark they approached the village of Melanson, on the bank of the Gaspereau. Each of the parties took possession of one of the houses, and in a short time the shivering men were enjoying the warmth of fires made in the great fireplaces of the Acadian peasants.

Where Coulon, the leader, found shelter, a wedding feast was going on. The arrival of these armed men, and the prospect of bloodshd, was a violent interruption to the happy proceedings. Do you say the Acadian peasants gave him information as to the English, and were, therefore, disloyal to their English masters? Perhaps so, but how long can a man hesitate with a bayonet at his breast? They had learned from bitter experience, from the armed forces of both sides, the lesson of yielding.

The English were quartered in twenty-four houses, scattered along a mile of the village street. Coulon realized that he took great chances unless he could make a simultaneous attack on all the houses, as the English outnumbered him. He had over three hundred men, so, dividing them into ten groups, he determined to make a simultaneous attack on the principal lodgments of the English, as his force was not large enough to attack them all at one time. The larger number, under his immediate command, was to be concentrated on the stone house occupied by Colonel Noble.

He quietly and stealthily marched through the blinding snow, and at two o'clock in the morning fell upon the unsuspecting and sleeping men. The sentinel fired his gun, but was instantly shot; and then began a massacre as merciless as any committed by the Indians for the time it lasted. The English fought valiantly, and only surrendered when half their number were dead or wounded. Coulon was wounded at the first fire from the house of Colonel Noble. Colonel Noble was shot twice, but continued to fire his pistols. The French called on him to surrender, but he refused, and in the next volley he was shot through the head and died instantly. The loss of the English was one hundred killed, one hundred and fifteen wounded, and fifty captured, while the French loss was seven killed and fifteen wounded.

CHAPTER XII.

In the summer of 1749 Edward Cornwallis was appointed Governor-General of Nova Scotia, and soon afterward arrived at Chebucto harbor, which had been discovered two years before. Here Halifax was founded, which became the seat of government in place of Annapolis. Halifax is about sixty miles southeast from the settlements at Minas, on one of the finest harbors in the world. From Halifax to the Acadian settlements at that time there was nothing but a trail. Roads were soon built under the direction of the Governor, and Cornwallis began his harsh and haughty rule over the Acadian peasants. The Acadian population at this time, according to the best authorities, English and French, numbered about ten thousand.

Cornwallis was called upon shortly after his arrival at Halifax by Claude Le Blanc, of Grand-Pré, and Jean Melanson, of Canard, representatives of the Acadian people, to pay their respects to the new Governor, and to ask to be permitted to remain as English subjects under the oath that they had taken years before under Phillips, namely, that they should not be required to take up arms against the French. They were given three months to take the oath or forfeit all their possessions.

The Governor's deputies were sent to ascertain the situation with reference to compliance with this order. They brought back the reply. It was a petition signed by more than a thousand inhabitants of Minas and the surrounding country asking to remain under the old oath, or be permitted to leave the country.

Cornwallis, finding them determined in standing out for the qualified oath, made harsh threats against them, which he, however, did not carry into execution. His attention soon became engrossed with the rapid growth and development of Halifax, so that the inhabitants of Grand-Pré remained, with few exceptions, on their farms. He wrote to the Lords of Trade that he hoped to make the Acadians as useful as possible as long as they remained. He also issued the following proclamation to the Acadians: " Whoever shall leave this Province without first taking the oath of allegiance, shall immediately forfeit all his rights."

The Neutrals were firm in their intention to leave the country rather than to take another oath which protected them neither from the excesses of the English officials and soldiery nor from the aggressions of the French and Indians. They were loth to leave their homes and cast their lot with the French, as, after having so long lived under English sovereignty there was no assurance that the French would treat them any better, yet the doubt and uncertainty of the next move by Cornwallis did not serve to assure them of better conditions under their present rulers.

It was at this time that the priest La Loutre, who seems to have been ever a disturbing element in the affairs of the Acadians, was guilty of an act of treachery which recoiled on the heads of the innocent peasants of Minas, and afforded another excuse for English severity.

La Loutre, who was working among the Micmacs and French at the isthmus, was unceasing in his efforts to have the Acadians leave their homes and join the French. On the isthmus were the two French forts, Beausejour and Gaspereau; on the opposite side of the river Misseguash was located the English fort, Lawrence. The French were enabled to reinforce and provision their garrisons from their settlements and forts in New Brunswick. There was more or less friction at all times between the garrisons of the two nations, and the machinations of La Loutre made matters worse. It was customary when any communication was to be had between the garrisons for officers of the contending forces to meet on neutral ground between the forts, under a flag of truce.

La Loutre dressed an Indian in the uniform of a French officer and sent him out under a flag of truce. Captain Howe, of the English garrison, saw the flag, and went in person to meet the supposed French officer; when he neared the Indian he was fired on from ambush by a party of Micmacs and instantly killed. With such sinister influences at work, and such violations of the laws of civilized warfare, it is not surpris-

ing that the government at Halifax looked with suspicion on all persons of French descent, and doubted
the good faith of the Acadians.

In the heat of passion and in the midst of such an
armed truce, men are not given to the nice discrimi-
nation and deliberate investigation which would
throw the light of truth on such affairs, but jump at
conclusions. Such was the case in the murder of
Captain Howe. The people of Minas, although far
from the scene of the tragedy, were considered
particeps criminis, and unjustly so, as after investigation has shown.

CHAPTER XIII.

We are now within two years or less of the final scene in the Acadian drama. Cornwallis was succeeded by Hopson, a man of noble character, wisdom and prudence. He was more humane than his predecessor, and bore no resemblance to the heartless, grasping Lawrence who followed him.

Could Hopson have remained at the head of the government at Halifax the foul blot of the Acadian expulsion would never have been thrown on the pages of American history. He saw at once the difficulty and unreasonableness of exacting, under existing conditions, the oath demanded by his predecessor. He knew how valuable to the country these people were, and could be made. The tone of his message to them shows clearly that he fully understood what had been the policy of the former government, and what treatment they had received at the hands of the soldiery. In his orders to the officers under him he says: " You are to look upon the Acadians in the same light with the rest of his Majesty's subjects, as to the protection of the laws and the government; for which reason nothing is to be taken from them by force, or any price set upon their goods but what they themselves agree to; and if at any time they should obstinately refuse to comply with what His Majesty's service may require of them, you are not to redress the wrong yourself by military force, or in any unlawful manner, but to lay the case before the Governor and await his orders. You are to cause the following orders to be stuck up in the most public part of the fort, both in English and French:

"'1. No provisions or any other commodities that the Acadians shall bring to the fort to sell are to be taken from them at any fixed price, but to be paid for according to a free agreement made between them and the purchasers.

"'2. No officer, non-commissioned officer or soldier shall presume to insult or otherwise abuse any of the Acadians, who are upon all occasions to be treated as His Majesty's subjects, and to whom the laws of the country are open, to protect as well as punish.'"

Peace, prosperity and happiness came to the Acadians under the beneficent and humane treatment of Governor Hopson. The population at this time under English rule was about ten thousand; half of this number belonged to the region generally known as " Minas," consisting of the settlements of Habitant, Gaspereau and Grand-Pré. Two churches, in separate parishes, were attended by the people of the villages and surrounding settlements, one at Grand-Pré and the other at Canard.

Here at this time we find the third generation of Acadians enjoying the rich fruits of their labors; the land, which had been reclaimed from the sea by means of dykes, yielded most bountifully. Coming up through generations of trials and harsh treatment they had learned the lesson of patience and forbearance. They, as well as their ancestors, had suffered and endured, yet all was not gloom. Even in the midst of the uncertainty which hung over them there were days and months of sunshine.

Haliburton, who was a resident of the territory, and who, it is known, had the opportunity of conversing with some of the older inhabitants, who are said to have witnessed the expulsion, says: " Their habitations, which were of wood, were extremely convenient, and furnished as neatly as substantial farmhouses in Europe. They raised a great deal of stock and poultry of all kinds, which made a wholesome variety in their foods. Their flocks were computed at from sixty to seventy thousand head, and most families had horses, though the farming or tillage was done with oxen." Their clothing was the product of their own wool and flax, raised on their farms and spun and woven into cloth by the dexterous housewives. Upon rare occasions some adorned themselves in the costly vestments of their French ancestors. " Real misery was unknown, and benevolence anticipated the demands of poverty. Every misfortune was relieved, as it were, before it was felt, without ostentation on the one hand or meanness on the other. It was, in short, a society of brethren, every individual of which was equally ready to give and receive what he thought just and fair."

The numerous fur-bearing animals of the region,

such as the fox, martin, wild-cat, bear, beaver and moose, furnished furs for the winter wear. Game in great abundance and variety furnished food, as well as sport for the hunter, while the rivers, bays and lakes were alive with the choicest of fish. In addition to raising stock on the pasture lands reclaimed from the sea, the soil, both here and on the uplands, produced an abundance of vegetables, as well as wheat, rye, flax and oats. The undyked lands produced grass which was much relished in the winter by the cattle. Orchards of the finest apple, peach, pear and cherry trees were planted on the uplands, and about the houses the smaller fruits were cultivated. They were in comfortable circumstances so far as their common needs were concerned. The strong ties of a common race, religion and kinship bound them together, and made of them one great family.

" Matrons and maidens sat in snow-white caps and in kirtles
    Scarlet and blue and green, with distaffs spinning the golden
    Flax for the gossiping looms, whose noisy shuttles within
       doors
    Mingled their sound with the whirr of the wheels and the
       songs of the maidens."

Their young men were possessed of a high sense of honor, integrity and morality, while their young women were pure, chaste, and possessed of all the traits of a noble womanhood. The long Acadian winter was filled with a round of innocent social pleasures, such as dancing, singing and many games common to the peasantry of France from whom they had descended.

Could we have entered an Acadian home on a winter night we would have found the big " back-log " in the generous fireplace, with a supply of wood piled high in the corner; the tongs, fire-shovel, and irons and crane, would have been in place, as they may yet be seen in some of our older farm-houses, although not in use. The mother and daughter at the spinning-wheel and loom, the father taking his evening smoke, while his sons are engaged in cleaning their rifles, mending a snow-shoe or some similar occupation.

Presently a neighbor drops in to discuss local affairs, the fears of further troubles with the English or French as the case may be, or the prospects for the next season's crop; others drop in, and the cider and apples and cake are passed around. The evening is passed in pleasant social intercourse. Bedtime arrives, and the guests take their departure, with mutual " God keep you through the night." It is a picture of rural America in the early days, read about in the story books, but now, alas! a thing of the past.

Governor-General Hopson was succeeded by Charles Lawrence. Lawrence had been a member of the Council since 1745, and was Lieutenant-Governor under Cornwallis and Hopson. He had been a major in the English army, was a keen, intelligent, unscrupulous, cruel and ambitious man. Much of the harshness of Cornwallis towards the Acadians was due to the vicious counsel of Lawrence. Harbin says: " His antecedents were humble, but he, being endowed

with more than ordinary ability, without the re-
straints of a refined or noble nature, gave way, when
opportunity offered for high purpose and manly
action, to the baser and more sordid impulses which
seem to have ruled his life. He was, moreover,
haughty and disdainful in manner. Without real
friends, his acts received support from his agents and
from those who were unable to resist him. Of low
cunning, a consummate flatterer of the higher, an
oppressor of the weak, with profuse use of false
promises, and every effort to accomplish his own personal ends, Lawrence has the unenviable distinction
of having caused the expatriation of the Acadians,
and of having done it with great cruelty."

"In the light of later facts thrown on their condition, it is almost beyond belief that a people should
be so patient and quietly persevering in their efforts
to remain upon their lands under all the impositions
practiced upon them. If individuals acted against the
peace of the country, a most cruel persecution followed the whole people, thinly disguised under
various pretexts. Their homes were their all, and
they bore insults and indignity for forty years in a
vain hope that a time would come when they would
be finally secure on the lands which their fathers had
taken from the sea and made beautiful and rich
beyond any in America."

Lawrence had become familiar with the rich lands
of the Acadians while he was a soldier doing duty in
this part of the country, and when he became Gov-

ernor he had fully made up his mind to get possession of them. To this end he trumped up false
charges against the Acadians. His first act was to
send a small detachment of soldiers from the garrison
at Halifax, and one hundred from Fort Edward, who
were distributed among the inhabitants, two to each
house, and at midnight they seized their arms, all
of which they could have had for the asking, and
placed them on a boat that lay in waiting at Grand-
Pré. He followed this seizure with a demand for all
others to bring in their arms. They at once obeyed.
The result was that almost five thousand were
secured.

Lawrence, up to this time, had not pressed the
question of the oath. He wanted the refusal to serve
as a good excuse for his later acts, and the time was
not yet ripe for their deportation. He was determined to make the conditions such that they would
refuse to take the oath, and he did this by changing
the oath to one which forced them to take up arms at
once against the French.

The inhabitants of Minas, and the other villages in
that section, addressed the following petition to the
Governor after the seizure of their arms:

"We, the inhabitants of Minas, Piziquid and the river
Canard, take the liberty of approaching your Excellency for
the purpose of testifying our sense of the care which the Government exercises over us. It appears, sir, that your Excellency doubts the sincerity with which we have promised to be
faithful to His Britannic Majesty. We most humbly beg your
Excellency to consider our past conduct. You will see that

6

very far from violating the oath we have taken, we have maintained it in its entirety, in spite of the solicitations and the
dreadful threats of another power. We will entertain, sir, the
same pure and sincere disposition to prove, under any circumstances, our unshaken fidelity to His Majesty, provided that
His Majesty shall allow us the same liberty that he has
granted us. We earnestly beg your Excellency to have the
goodness to inform us of His Majesty's intentions on this subject, and to give us assurances on his part.

" Permit us, if you please, sir, to make known the annoying
circumstances in which we are placed, to the prejudice of the
tranquillity we ought to enjoy. Under pretext that we are
transporting our corn or other provisions to Beausejour and
the River St. John, we are no longer permitted to carry the
least quantity of corn by water from one place to another.
We beg your Excellency to be assured that we have never
transported provisions to Beausejour or to the River St. John.
If some refugee inhabitants from Beausejour have been seized
with cattle, we are not on that account by any means guilty,
inasmuch as the cattle belonged to them as private individuals,
and they were driving them to their respective habitations.
As to ourselves, sir, we have never offended in that respect, and
consequently we ought not, in our opinion, to be punished; on
the contrary, we hope that your Excellency will be pleased to
restore to us the same liberty that we enjoyed formerly, in
giving us the use of our canoes, either to transport our goods
from one river to another, or for the purpose of fishing; there-
by providing for our livelihood. This permission has never
been taken from us except at the present time.

" We hope, sir, that you will be pleased to restore it, spe-
cially in consideration of the number of poor inhabitants who
would be very glad to support their families with the fish they
would be able to catch. Moreover, our guns, which we regard
as our own personal property, have been taken from us, notwithstanding the fact that they are absolutely necessary to us
to defend our cattle which are attacked by wild beasts, or for
the protection of our children and ourselves.

" Any inhabitant who may have his oxen in the woods, and
who may need them for purposes of labor, would not dare

expose himself in going for them without being prepared to defend himself. It is certain, sir, that since the Indians have ceased frequenting our parts, the wild beasts have greatly increased, and that our cattle are devoured by them almost every day. Besides, the arms which have been taken from us are but a feeble guarantee of our fidelity. It is not the gun which an inhabitant possesses that will make him more faithful; but his conscience alone must induce him to maintain his oath. An order has appeared in your Excellency's name, given at Fort Edward, June 24th, 1755, by which we are commanded to carry guns, pistols, etc., etc., to Fort Edward. It appears to us, sir, that it would be dangerous for us to execute that order before representing to you the danger to which this order exposes us. The Indians may come and threaten and plunder us, reproaching us for having furnished arms to kill them. We hope, sir, that you will be pleased, on the contrary, to order that those taken from us be restored to us. By so doing you will afford us the means of preserving both ourselves and our cattle.

"In the last place, we are grieved, sir, at seeing ourselves declared guilty without being aware of having disobeyed. One of our inhabitants of the River Canard, named Pierre Melanson, was seized and arrested in charge of his boat, before having heard of any order forbidding that sort of transport. We beg your Excellency, on this subject, to have the goodness to make known to us your good pleasure before confiscating our property and considering us in fault. This is the favor we expect from your Excellency's kindness, and we hope you will do us the justice to believe that, very far from violating our promises, we will maintain them; assuring you that we are,

"Very respectfully, sir, your humble and obedient servants."

To the above petition the Governor replied as follows:

"The memorial of the 10th of June is highly arrogant and insidious, and deserves the highest resentment."

On the 24th of June a second petition was sent, in which they apologized for anything they may have said, and disclaimed any intention of being without respect for the Government. This was signed by forty-four inhabitants, representing the people of Minas, Canard and Piziquid. The delegates bearing this petition appeared before the Governor, whereupon he gave them twenty-four hours in which to take an oath in which it was now expressly set forth that they were to bear arms against the French. The delegates begged to be permitted to return and consult with their people. This the Governor refused, and on the following day he asked for their answer. They replied that they could give no answer without first consulting with their people. They were now treated as prisoners of war.

On the 5th of July one hundred more delegates called upon Lawrence, and begged for the release of their imprisoned fellows: " Charity for our detained inhabitants and their innocents oblige us to beg your Excellency to be touched by our miseries and restore to them their liberty, with possible submission and profound respect." To this petition Lawrence replied with the question, " Will you or will you not swear to the King of Great Britain that you will take up arms against the King of France, his enemy ? " The answer was not less laconic than the question. " Since," they said, " we are asked only for a yes or no we will answer unanimously, No," adding, however, that what was required of them tended to despoil them of their religion and everything else.

Immediately the Governor gave orders to transport them to a small island, distant as far as a cannon-ball would carry from Halifax, whither they were conducted like criminals, and where they remained until the end of October, fed on a little bread, and deprived of the possibility of receiving any assistance as well as of speaking to any one.

The Governor imagined that this harshness would soften their courage; he found them as firm as ever. He took the resolution of betaking himself to the aforesaid island with a numerous retinue, accompanied by all the instruments of torture, in order to try to soften their courage at the sight of this spectacle. In the midst of this display, befitting a tyrant, he asked them if they persisted in their answers. One of them replied, " Yes, and more than ever; we have God for us, and that is enough." The Governor drew his sword and said, " Insolent fellow; you deserve that I should run my sword through your body." The peasant presented his breast to him, and, drawing nearer, said, " Strike, if you dare; I shall be the first martyr of the band; you can kill my body, but you shall not kill my soul." The Governor, in a sort of frenzy, asked the others if they shared the feelings of " that insolent fellow," who had just spoken. All with one voice exclaimed, " Yes, sir; yes, sir."

The whole trend of Lawrence's acts up to this time had been in keeping with his well-defined and settled plan of driving the Acadians from their homes.

CHAPTER XIV.

THE EXPULSION.

" Four days now are passed since the English ships at their anchors
Ride in the Gaspereau's mouth, with their cannon pointed against us.
What their design may be is unknown ; but all are commanded
On the morrow to meet in the church, where his Majesty's mandate
Will be proclaimed as law in the land. Alas ! in the meantime
Many surmises of evil alarm the hearts of the people."

We now come to the climax in the drama which
forms the basis of Longfellow's " Evangeline." In
August, 1755, an expedition under the command of
Colonel Robert Monckton, an English officer, but
composed largely of New England troops (about fifteen hundred), under Colonel Winslow, was sent to
capture the French forts. Winslow captured Fort
Beausejour, and a few weeks later became the chief
instrument for the forcible removal of the Acadian
peasants.

He now took up his quarters at Grand-Pré to await
the arrival of the transports which were on their way
from Boston, where Governor Lawrence had quietly
made arrangements for hiring them. The Council,
under Lawrence, and those officers who were sworn
to secrecy with him, decided " to remove all the
French inhabitants out of the Province, if they
refused to take the oath." At a meeting of this
Council, July 28th, " after mature consideration it
was unanimously agreed that to prevent as much as
possible their attempting to return to molest the settlers that may be set down on their lands, it would be

most proper to send them to be distributed amongst the several colonies on the continent, and that a sufficient number of vessels should be hired with all possible expedition for that purpose . . . and dispose of them as best suits our design in preventing their reunion."

Lawrence's final orders were that " the inhabitants must be collected by force or stratagem, not paying any attention to any remonstrance or memorial from any inhabitant whatever, who may be desirous of staying behind, but to embark every person according to instructions sent." Upon the arrival of the vessels, as many of the inhabitants as could be collected by any means, particularly the heads of families and young men, were to be shipped on board of them at the rate of two persons per ton burthen of the vessels. They were to be supplied with five pounds of flour and one pound of pork, to be delivered to each person so shipped to last seven days. The men in charge of the vessels were charged to use every precaution to prevent the captives from seizing the vessels, and were not to allow many on deck at the same time, and that they be sure that all are without arms or weapons of any kind.

Everything was now in readiness. The vessels were already collecting in the Basin of Minas. Winslow was scouring the country in all directions with his officers, to become familiar with the situation. The correspondence between Colonel Winslow, Governor Lawrence and Captain Murray in reference to the Acadians, and the scheme for their dispersion, is most interesting; in it can be read on, as well as between the lines, the heartless conspiracy against the Acadians.

Halifax was a growing English town, and this fertile inland country was needed to supply the ever-growing demands of the garrison and the people. Winslow, in one of his letters to Governor Lawrence, says: " Adams and party returned this morning from their march to the River Canard, and reported it was a fine country, full of inhabitants, and a beautiful church; abundance of the goods of this world and provisions of all kinds in plenty." Of the visit to the villages of Melanson and River Gaspereaux he says: " Both parties which returned this evening gave each an account that it was a fine country." And yet this fine and beautiful country, with its churches, homes, villages, farms, grain, fruit and live stock, was soon to be devastated, and its unsuspecting inhabitants scattered far and wide among a strange and unfriendly people.

Captain Murray, who was at Fort Edward (now Windsor) writes to Colonel Winslow:

"I was out yesterday at the villages. All the people were quite busy at the harvest. If this day keeps fair, all will be in here into their barns. I hope to-morrow will crown all our wishes.   " Yours most truly, etc.,
                                          " MURRAY."

Winslow held a consultation with Captain Murray at Fort Edward, and on September 2d, issued the following citation:

Gaspereau River (Falmouth in distance).

"WHEREAS, His Excellency, the Governor, has instructed us of his late resolution respecting the matter proposed to the inhabitants, and has ordered us to communicate the same in person, His Excellency being desirous that each of them should be satisfied of His Majesty's intentions, which he has also ordered us to communicate to you, as they have been given to him: We therefore order and strictly, by these presents, all of the inhabitants of the above-named districts, both old and young men as well as the lads of ten years of age, to attend at the Church at Grand-Pré, on Friday the 5th instant, at three in the afternoon, that we may impart to them, that we were ordered to communicate to them, declaring that no excuse will be admitted on any pretence whatever on the pain of forfeiting goods and chattels, in default of real estate.

"Given at Grand-Pré, 2nd Septembre, 1755.

"JOHN WINSLOW."

Less than three days intervened between the citation of Colonel Winslow and the ever memorable 5th of September, which sealed the fate of thousands of thrifty, frugal and peaceable people. On this day they were to meet in the sacred edifice in which they had so often met for divine worship, a church hallowed by all the ties and associations sacred to a simple and devout people, there to receive a message, the purport of which they were entirely ignorant, and whose consequences they were wholly unprepared to meet. Until the last few hours of that day many of the unsuspecting peasantry were employed gathering in their harvests and making all the necessary preparations for the coming winter. Indeed, there were not a few who hoped that now, with a strong garrison in their midst to protect them, their trials were at last to come to an end. This delusion was dispelled a few hours later. Little did they dream, as they gathered about their firesides on the evening of the 4th of September, that to many families it was the last reunion. They wondered at and discussed the latest citation; young and old were prepared to obey it. In some homes were the aged, infirm and dying; in others the joy and happiness of youth, the joy of the young father and mother as they gaze on the tiny first-born as it lies smiling in its rude wooden cradle. There may have been dark forebodings of coming ill, but not the wildest imagination could grasp the terrible reality. Citations and orders were not new to them, and they had always obeyed them to the letter; what the morrow meant for them they did not know, but surely nothing worse than what had preceded. It might be that His Majesty had decided to grant their petitions and restore to them their arms and boats, and allow them the free use of both, or it might mean additional restrictions, but deportation, never.

" Pleasantly rose next morn the sun on the village of Grand-
      Pré.
  Pleasantly gleamed in the soft, sweet air the Basin of Minas,
  Where the ships, with their wavering shadows, were riding
      at anchor.
  Life had long been astir in the village, and clamorous labor
  Knocked with its hundred hands at the golden gates of the
      morning.
  Now from the country around, from the farms and neighbor-
      ing hamlets,
  Came in their holiday dresses, the blithe Acadian peasants."

Old Well and Willows in Front of Church, Grand-Pré.

The morning of the 5th of September dawned bright and clear; the sun shone with a splendor befitting this cool northern climate; the brown thrush was singing his farewell in the orchard, and the quail was whistling his " bob white " down in the meadow; the migratory birds were heading for warmer climes, while the crow from his lofty tree was cawing in mocking glee over his sole possession of the land through the long and dreary winter fast approaching. The chores and household duties were attended to with the accustomed care and regularity, and in many households preparations were made for an early start for Grand-Pré, as some had many miles to go to reach the place of gathering.

Old men, young men and boys wended their way from Canard, Pereau, Habitant, from the Gaspereau valley, Avonport and all the villages of Minas, by the roads converging on Grand-Pré. Four hundred and eighteen men, the sturdy sons of toil, clad in their rough, but clean and neat homespun clothes, entered the church of St. Charles at the appointed hour. It was in this church that they had been christened and many of them married. Here, too, they had received the Holy Sacrament. Winslow records in his journal that " at three in the afternoon the French inhabitants appeared, agreeable to their citation, at the church in Grand-Pré, amounting to four hundred and eighteen of their best men: upon which I ordered a table to be set in the center of the church, and having

attended with those of my officers who were off
guard, delivered to them by interpreters the King's
orders."

"Gentlemen: I have received from His Excellency, Governor
Lawrence, the King's commission, which I have in my hands;
and by his orders you are convened together to manifest to
you His Majesty's final resolution to the French inhabitants
of this Province of Nova Scotia: who for almost a half century
have had more indulgence granted them than any other of his
subjects in any part of his dominions: what use you have
made of it, you yourselves best know. The part of duty I am
now upon, though necessary, is very disagreeable to my make
and temper, as I know it must be grievous to you, who are of
the same species; but it is not my business to animadvert, but
to obey such orders as I receive, and therefore, without hesita-
tion, shall deliver you His Majesty's orders and instructions;
namely—that your lands and tenements, cattle of all kinds
and live stock of all sorts, are forfeited to the crown; with all
other your effects, saving your money and household goods and
yourselves, to be removed from this Province. Thus it is per-
emptorily His Majesty's orders, that the whole French inhabitants in these districts be removed: and I am, through His
Majesty's goodness, directed to allow you liberty to carry off
your money and household goods, as many as you can without
discommoding the vessels you go in. I shall do everything in
my power that all these goods be secured to you, and that you
are not molested in carrying them off: and also that whole
families shall go in the same vessels, and make this remove,
which I am sensible must make you a great deal of trouble, as
easy as his Majesty's service will admit; and hope that in
whatever part of the world you may fall, you may be faithful subjects, a peaceable and happy people. I must also inform
you that it is His Majesty's pleasure that you remain in security under the inspection and direction of the troops I have
the honor to command."

The blow had fallen;—a bolt of lightning from a
clear sky. The men were stupefied, dazed; the awful-

ness of their fate slowly impressed itself upon them. They were prisoners in their own church, surrounded by hostile troops, and separated from their wives and children.

The words of Winslow, although couched in as mild terms as his language would admit, yet contained no words of hope or cheer. Their destination was not even pointed out to them. All that they were certain of was that they were being despoiled of their homes and the fruits of the labors of three generations of hard-working, industrious and frugal ancestors; that they were to go out into a strange world poverty-stricken and friendless. The bulk of their property was in their farms and flocks;—of money they had little.

Winslow, after delivering the edict of banishment, retired to the parish house, which he had been occupying since his arrival at Grand-Pré. Some of the older Acadians besought him to consider the condition of their families, and allow a small delegation of men to return to their homes and let their people know of their sad condition. Finally, after consultation with his officers, he permitted ten to return each day for the five days intervening between their imprisonment and the first embarcation, the 10th of September.

Winslow closes the day's business with the following remarks in his journal: " The French people not having with them any provisions, and many of them pleading hunger, begged for bread, on which I gave them, and ordered that for the future they be supplied from their respective families. Thus ended the memorable 5th day of September, a day of great fatigue and trouble."

Thus ended the day so far as Winslow was concerned, but how about the poor wretches imprisoned in the church, and those at home who were anxiously awaiting their return? One would like to draw the curtain and hide from view the sorrow and mental suffering of the next few days, but the historian and the poet have long since given to the world the story. The news spread rapidly to each and every fireside, where, with anxious solicitude, mothers and children were awaiting the return of fathers, sons and brothers.

We can imagine their consternation when late in the evening they were apprised of their terrible fate.

Contrary to all expectation of their persecutors, they received their sentence and bore their incarceration with a fortitude and resignation befitting Christian martyrs. If all history were silent as to the peaceable character of the Acadians, no better evidence would be needed than their heroic conduct at this time. To all pleas to be permitted to visit their families, assist those who needed their care, and to gather together their worldly effects, Winslow turned a deaf ear, except to permit ten men each day, out of four hundred and eighteen, to return, and this for five days.

During the next few days the soldiers scoured the

country in all directions in search of those who had not reported at Grand-Pré. Under this pretext, and the license granted them by Lawrence, they searched the houses, appropriated to their own use what they desired, and destroyed what they could not carry off. Women were insulted, scoffed at and maltreated, and in some instances outraged. Lawrence had not only given his soldiers license, but positive orders, to " distress them as much as possible."

For three days wains loaded with the goods and effects of the peasants were being drawn to the landing, a mile or more below the church, and " here on the bank lay in confusion the household goods of the peasants." " All over the country dense clouds of smoke arose to the sky as the sun was sinking in the west, and later the heavens were aglow with the light from hundreds of burning buildings. The cows returning burdened with milk patiently and piteously called for the milk-maid to perform her daily task and thus give relief; the horses whinnying for their food; the chickens cackling and crowing, startled by the unusual glare; the bellowing of cattle, enveloped in flames; the cries and moans of distressed women and children, all added to the horror of a scene without a parallel in American history."

In the Basin of Minas already lay five transports, with nine more to come. According to the order, two thousand persons were to be shipped from Minas, and the distribution was to be as follows: To North Carolina, five hundred; to Virginia, one thousand; to

Maryland, five hundred, or in proportion if the number to be shipped off should exceed two thousand persons. Of the transports assembled at Annapolis the distribution was as follows: To be sent to Philadelphia, such a number as will transport three hundred persons; to New York, sufficient to transport two hundred persons; to Connecticut, sufficient to transport three hundred persons, and to Boston, such a number of vessels as will transport two hundred persons, or rather more in proportion to Connecticut, should the number to be shipped off exceed one thousand.

CHAPTER XV.

THE EMBARKATION.

Thus to the Gaspereau's mouth they hurried and there on the sea-beach
Piled in confusion lay the household goods of the peasants.
All day long between the shore and the ships did the boats ply;
All day long the wains came laboring down from the village.
Late in the afternoon when the sun was near to his setting,
Echoed far o'er the fields came the roll of drums from the churchyard.
Thither the women and children thronged. On a sudden the churchdoors
Opened, and forth came the guard, and marching in gloomy procession
Followed the long-imprisoned, but patient, Acadian farmers.
Even as pilgrims, who journey afar from their homes and their country,
Sing as they go, and in singing forget they are weary and wayworn,
So with songs on their lips the Acadian peasants descended
Down from the church to the shore, amid their wives and their daughters.

On the 10th of the month the first loading of the
transports began. The five days' imprisonment and
separation from their loved ones, the intense strain
upon their nerves, and the mental anguish, had by
this time begun to tell on the prisoners. Winslow,
noticing the restlessness manifested among them,
became somewhat alarmed, and concluded to place
fifty men on each transport then at anchor in the bay
and thus lessen the danger. Summoning their leader,
Pierre Landry, who spoke English, Winslow ac-
quainted him with his intention of embarking two
hundred and fifty of the men and boys. Landry
pleaded with him not to separate the children and
young men from their parents, and husbands from
their wives, but to permit them to go together, and
to give them time to collect their goods. He and
others petitioned Winslow to be permitted to go
among his people, and that they themselves would
pay all the expense.

7

Their pleadings were in vain. Winslow turned a deaf ear to all their appeals, and sternly ordered the guard to draw up in line to enforce his command that all " unmarried men and boys should form six deep and be marched to the landing."

There were eighty soldiers under Captain Adams in charge of this contingent. The command was given to march, but, overwhelmed with grief at the thought of being separated from their families and parents, they refused to move. Cries of grief and anger, mingled with tears and pleadings for mercy, prayers and petitions, rent the balmy air of that bright September day. All that they asked was that Colonel Winslow would carry out his promise, made in the church on the day of their incarceration, that families should not be separated.

The next command was: " Fix bayonets— Charge ! "—a most powerful incentive to move unarmed men. And now began one of the saddest processions the bright sun of heaven ever looked down upon. From the church they moved down the road to the landing, singing hymns, praying and crying as each might be affected. On either side of the road stood their mothers, sisters and sweethearts, wringing their hands in despair. The same scene was repeated when the older men were marched down to the boats, until the entire male population of Minas was on board the transports. The number embarked the first day was two hundred and thirty.

" All day the boats plied between the ships and

Grand-Pré Meadows.

The willows mark the site of the Acadian village of Grand-Pré.

the shore." This expression is better understood
when we remember that the tides in the Bay of
Fundy and the Basin of Minas rise from thirty to
sixty feet, and that at low tide the vessels were some
miles out in the basin. On the shore, without home
or shelter, crouched the women and children about
their few household goods; there, too, were the aged
and infirm, many forced from beds of sickness to die
on the sands of the shore, and there be hastily buried.

" Thus to the Gaspereau's mouth moved on that mournful pro-
    cession.
  There disorder prevailed, and the tumult and stir of embark-
    ing.
  Busily plied the freighted boats; and in the confusion
  Wives were torn from their husbands, and mothers, too late,
    saw their children
  Left on the land, extending their arms, with wildest en-
    treaties.
  So unto separate ships were Basil and Gabriel carried."

It was the 8th of October before the final embarcation took place, owing to the delay in getting transports. The entire country, with the exception of
Grand-Pré, had been desolated, and the houses and
barns of the people burned; those at Grand-Pré were
destroyed later in the fall, when the soldiers left the
place. Winslow says in his journal: " On the 8th
we began to embark the inhabitants, who went off
sullenly and unwillingly, the women in great distress,
carrying off their children in their arms; others carrying their decrepit parents in their carts, with all their
goods, moving in great confusion, and it appeared a

scene of woe and distress." In the confusion and haste, naturally complicated by the difference in language, and the utter disregard on the part of the officers to listen to the appeals of the unfortunates, " wives were torn from their husbands, and mothers too late saw their children left on the land, extending their arms in wildest entreaty."

Colonel Winslow went to Fort Edward, fifteen miles farther east, where the people were gathered together from Habitant and Canard Rivers, ready for embarkation from Budro's Point. Similar scenes were enacted here, but the few vessels sent to this point were hardly sufficient to accommodate the people, much less their goods, and the latter were left on the shore.

Six years later, when the English began to settle upon the rich and fertile lands of the people whom they had displaced and dispersed, the broken and decayed remains of carts, wagons, furniture, etc., found on the shore were all that was left to tell the story of the once happy Acadian occupation.

I cannot close this chapter better than with a quotation from Herbin: " I shall not dwell on this closing scene of the Acadian occupation of Grand-Pré and Minas. Harsh words are useless. The chief designer, Lawrence, has been stigmatized as having brought about the deportation of the Acadians. Of the same blood and race as these exiles, I have been a dweller of Minas for thirteen years. My home has been in the midst of the dykes and marshes, in sight of the Grand-Pré, the Basin of Minas. I have visited a great part of the country of Minas once occupied by the Acadians. The willows, set out by them, mark the sites of many of their former villages. Their orchards still bear fruit, and their cellar walls yet mark the places where they lived and died, and from which hundreds were driven to leave their bones in other places. My ancestors found their way back to Nova Scotia, and settled on the shores of St. Mary's Bay, where their numerous descendants are to-day. By some strange chance I am here, the only Acadian of whom I know living amid the same scenes that knew the people of Minas from 1671 to 1755."

CHAPTER XVI.

THE ACADIAN IN EXILE.

Many a weary year had passed since the burning of Grand-Pré,
When on the falling tide the freighted vessels departed,
Bearing a nation, with all its household gods, into exile,
Exile without an end, and without an example in story.
Far asunder on separate coasts, the Acadians landed,
Scattered were they, like flakes of snow, when the wind from the northeast
Strikes aslant through the fogs that darken the Banks of Newfoundland.
Friendless, homeless, hopeless, they wandered from city to city.
Asked of the earth but a grave, and no longer a friend nor a fireside.

To follow these people in their wanderings as
exiles would be but to lengthen the story of their
sufferings. The people of the colonies were unwilling
to receive among them " so undesirable and dangerous a foe," for such Lawrence had proclaimed them
to be, particularly when the military forces were
needed on the western frontier. Furthermore, in
some of the colonies at this time the religious senti-
ment was very bitter against anything that savored
of papacy. The struggles between Protestant and
Catholic, which had deluged the old world with its
best blood for years was forcibly reflected in the
colonies. The distrust of the Acadian was due to his
religion, nationality, and the highly-colored and sen-
sational reports put forth by Lawrence to justify his
outrageous act of deportation. The colonies were
at times engaged in a war with the French and Indians, and did not draw a very fine distinction between
a Frenchman and a French " Neutral." At all events
they did not want the Acadians. Lawrence had been
shrewd enough to keep his intentions from the gov-

ernors of the several colonies, and simply dropped his cargoes down upon them.

Three vessels loaded with their cargoes of human freight anchored in the Delaware River, just below Philadelphia, on the 20th of November. Governor Morris refused to allow them to land, and for a period of two months or more they were forced to remain on board. Many of them died, and their bodies were secretly consigned to the river. They were fed on a meager diet of flour and pork, so that when at last they were permitted to land, they were so weak and famished that out of four hundred and fifty originally consigned to Pennsylvania, two hundred and thirty-three had died. They were kindly received by the people of Philadelphia, notwithstanding the Governor's seeming harshness.

Watson, in his " Annals of Philadelphia," says: " The part which came to Philadelphia were provided with quarters in a long range of one-story wooden houses, built on the north side of Pine Street, and extending from Fifth to Sixth Streets. . . . These Neutrals remained there several years, showing very little disposition to amalgamate and settle with our society, or attempting any good for themselves. They made a French town in the midst of our society, and were content to live spiritless and poor. Finally they made themselves burdensome, so that the authorities, to awaken them to more sensibility, determined in the year 1757 to have their children bound out by the Overseers of the Poor, alleging as their reason that the parents had lived long enough at the public expense. It soon after occurred that they all went off in a body to the banks of the Mississippi, near New Orleans, where their descendants may still be found, under the general name of Arcadians [Acadians], an easy, gentle, happy, but lowly, people."

The humane and pious Anthony Benezet was their kind friend, and did whatever he could to ameliorate their situation. He educated many of their daughters, and his charities to them were constant and unremitting." A few found homes among some of the Huguenot families of the city and state. Governor Morris, of Pennsylvania, was very much concerned about the presence of the Acadians in the Province, and addressed a note to Governor Shirley, of Massachusetts, concerning the matter. He says: " Two vessels are arrived here with upwards of three hundred Neutral French from Nova Scotia, whom Governor Lawrence has sent to remain in this Province, and I am at a very great loss to know what to do with them. The people here, as there is no military force of any kind, are very uneasy at the thought of having a number of enemies scattered among the very bowels of the country, who may go off from time to time with intelligence, and join their countrymen now employed against us, or foment some intestine commotion in conjunction with the Irish and German Catholics, in this and the neighboring Province. I therefore must beg your particular instructions in what manner I may best dispose of these people, as I am desirous of doing anything that may contribute to His Majesty's service. I have in the meantime put a guard, out of the recruiting parties now in town, on board of each of the vessels, and ordered these Neutrals to be supplied with provisions, which must be at the expense of the Crown, as I have no Provincial money in my hands for this service. I have prevailed on Captain Morris, who is recruiting here for Colonel Dunbar's regiment, to postpone sending off his recruits till I hear from you upon this head, which I hope by return of post."

The Governor of New Jersey was even more pronounced in his antagonism and fears. He calls them " rebels " and " recusants," and is surprised at the Government sending them to the colonies, and would do all he could to prevent their landing in his State, etc. A Philadelphia paper of the time contained the following: " A few days since three Frenchmen were taken up and imprisoned on suspicion of having poisoned some wells in the neighborhood. They are not yet tried, and it is imagined if they are convicted thereof they will have but a few hours to live after they are once condemned." The fears of the people among whom the Acadians were distributed seem ridiculous to us at this time, but they were in the midst of a war which was desolating the frontiers of Virginia, Pennsylvania and New York, and the English and colonial arms had not at that time been successful. In their stay of something over two years in Philadelphia they never made any attempt to help themselves; they begged to be treated as prisoners of war, and sent back to Acadia or to France. They seem to have been utterly heart-broken and despondent.

In one of their memorials to the Assembly of the Province they say: " We bless God that it was our lot to be sent to Pennsylvania, where our wants have been relieved, and we have in every respect been treated with Christian benevolence and charity." Again: "We humbly pray that you would extend your goodness so far as to give us leave to depart from hence, or be pleased to send us to our nation, or anywhere to join our country-people; but if you cannot grant us these favors, we desire that provisions be made for our subsistence as long as we are detained here. If this our humble request should be refused, and our wives and children be suffered to perish before our eyes, how grievous this will be. Had we not better died in our native land ? "

Their reception in Maryland was about the same accorded them in all the other colonies. Governor Dulany says that they insisted on being treated as prisoners of war, and that they had to be maintained at the public expense. " They have eaten us up. Political considerations may make this deportation a prudent step, for anything I know, and perhaps their behavior may have deservedly brought their suffering upon them, but it is impossible not to compassionate their sufferings."

In Virginia, Governor Dinwiddie received them with alarm. Virginia had taken an active part in the war; her own leader, Washington, had been defeated, and matters were very uncertain on the frontier. The prospect was certainly not encouraging, and to have quartered among them a lot of French as prisoners of war, or in any other relation, was not pleasing to the Governor or his people. He managed to maintain them until the meeting of the Assembly, and then ordered them shipped to England, at an expense of eight thousand pounds. They were not allowed to leave their ships, and many of them died before they set sail for England. A few out of the consignment of fifteen hundred for this colony were sent north.

In the Carolinas and Georgia they were probably less welcome than elsewhere. Governor Glen sent fifty or more to Virginia, but Dinwiddie sent these farther north. Jones, in his history of Georgia, says: "They went scattering all over the country." Some of these probably found their way to Louisiana. Of the ships containing the consignment of fifteen hundred for England, some were lost at sea, and it is estimated that over four hundred perished. A severe storm drove the other ships to San Domingo. A few reached England, and were eventually shipped to France.

The fifteen hundred who were shipped to South Carolina were given permission to construct boats, in which they coasted along the Atlantic coast, in efforts to return. After untold hardships, a small number succeeded in reaching St. John's, New Brunswick. Others from Georgia, and those banished from the Carolinas, were slowly making their way up the coast, when Lawrence, hearing of it, sent a letter to the Governors of New York and Massachusetts, ordering them to seize the Acadians' ships and destroy them. This order was obeyed. Some were seized at the east end of Long Island and on the Connecticut coast, and others at the entrance to Boston harbor.

Lawrence, in one of his letters to the Governor of Massachusetts says: " As to the conduct of the southern colonies in permitting those who were removed to coast along from one province to another, in order that they might get back to Nova Scotia, nothing is more blamable; and had not the Governors of New York and Massachusetts Bay prudently stopped them, there is no attempt, however desperate and cruel, which might not have been expected from persons exasperated as they must have been with the treatment they had received."

Over one thousand landed at various times at Charleston, and they were dispersed among the several counties, " for the public safety," as it was alleged. The Legislature passed a law with reference to these exiles similar to that of Pennsylvania. They eventually left the Province, with the exception of one family, which embraced the Protestant faith, and whose descendants are still to be found in Charleston.

CHAPTER XVII.

Most of the Acadians consigned to the New England colonies landed at Boston. Here two thousand, after considerable delay, were landed from the foul crafts in which they had been shipped, and were given temporary quarters on Boston Common, and afterwards distributed among the surrounding towns. They were not permitted to visit any of their kindred or friends in adjoining towns, under the penalty of ten lashes and five days' imprisonment. They were subjected to the most rigid surveillance. All the crimes committed in the neighborhood were charged to the Acadians.

The Massachusetts records show that until 1766 vessels continued to bring exiles to Boston, until the Legislature absolutely put a stop to it. In the meantime Colonel Winslow quarreled with Lawrence, and was no longer willing to countenance his acts of cruelty, particularly since he was forced to witness at his own home the sufferings of the exiles, and realized that he was in a measure responsible for their pitiable condition.

All these years soldiers were scouring the forests of Acadia for any who might have escaped the several deportations, or who might have returned. They were hunted like wild beasts. A number of them had taken refuge in the islands and bays in and about Cape Sable, at the time of the expulsion from Annapolis. Here they managed to eke out a miserable existence by hunting and fishing, and the few vegetables they were able to raise. They lived in constant terror of capture. Lawrence, hearing that some had escaped and were taking refuge in this part of the Peninsula, ordered Major Peeble, who was about to return with some of the New England troops to Boston, to stop and seize them and burn their huts. One historian says, to the credit of Peeble, that he refused to carry out the orders. Another writer says that he did obey orders to the extent of burning their huts. Be this as it may, it is a fact that in 1758 this remnant at Cape Sable petitioned the " Honorable Council at Boston," asking to be permitted to remain where they were, under their protection; or if that could not be granted, they asked to be taken to New England, and they would pay taxes and help maintain the war against France. They numbered forty families, or about one hundred and fifty persons all told. " Dear sirs," they petitioned, " do for us what lies in your power to settle us here, and we will be your faithful subjects until death." A year later Lawrence sent an armed vessel to Cape Sable. One hundred and fifty of the refugees were made prisoners, their houses were burned, and they were taken to Halifax and imprisoned on an island in the harbor which only a few years before had been the scene of

Lawrence's brutality to seventy of the inhabitants of Minas.

Death, the friend of the Acadian, as of the poor, claimed his share of these. The few who survived were sent to England. England herself complained of the shipment, and sent them to France, where to-day their descendants " inhabit two communes, wherein the peaceful habitudes and rustic peculiarities of their race are still recognizable among the verdant oases which dot the moorlands of Gascony in France."

CHAPTER XVIII.

Peace having been declared (1763) between the mother countries, the Acadian refugees started on their weary march back to New Brunswick and Nova Scotia. Over eight hundred left Boston at one time, tramping in all kinds of weather through the forests of Maine, along the north shore of the Bay of Fundy, in New Brunswick, up to the Isthmus of Shediac, north of the Basin of Minas. Here they halted, for, peering across the Basin, they beheld another people in possession of their lands. For months and years they had wended their toilsome way, weary, hungry and shelterless, but ever with the fond hope of regaining their native land. Some halted in the southern part of New Brunswick, and began erecting huts; others went into the northern part of the Province and settled at Madawaska; still others continued their weary way across the isthmus to Fort Beausejour (now New Cumberland), around the shores of Minas, Piziquid and Grand-Pré.

On through what had been the village of Grand-Pré, through the Cornwallis valley, down the Annapolis valley to Annapolis, down to the shores of St. Mary's Bay, went fifty or sixty poor wretches, the remnant of a once happy and contented people. What a flood of recollections must have crowded upon

Cornwallis.

them as they stood gazing on the ruins of their once happy homes! What emotions of joy, mingled with anguish and despair!—the land of their birth, the home of their childhood! The orchards, the willows and the poplars were still standing, as they are to-day, but the homes were gone and their farms were in the possession of others.

" Still stands the forest primeval; but under the shade of its branches
  Dwells another race, with other customs and language."

The willows and orchards—these same old landmarks—were all that whispered a welcome to the poor exiles, whose requiem they had sung only eight years before. They stood as the proud monuments of the Acadian farmer's planting and care;—little changed, excepting that they, too, had grown riper in years, broken with the storms of war and winter. Some were dead and decaying, each telling its tale of the sad scenes enacted in this land of sunshine and plenty.

How changed the scene! Here the ruins of their church, sacred to them through the observance of the rites of their religion,—the sacrament, the christening of their babes, and the solemnization of their marriage vows. There the old well that often quenched alike the thirst of priest and flock. On all sides nothing but destruction and desolation greeted them. Was this their beloved Acadia ?

The English inhabitants of this section looked on them with a species of horror. The children were

8

frightened by them, the men and women were annoyed as by a threatening specter from the grave; everybody was angry with them, and the poor wretches dragged themselves from village to village, worried and worn out by fatigue, cold, hunger and despair, that grew at every halting-place, till at last they reached the deserted shore of St. Mary's Bay, a barren and desolate stretch of country on the north-west coast of Nova Scotia. Here, under necessity, these unfortunate outcasts raised log huts; took to fishing and hunting; began to clear the land, and soon, out of the felled trees, some roughly-built houses were put up. Here their offspring, down through many generations, still live.

Although the treaty of peace between England and France was signed in 1763, and the Acadians were working their way back to Canada and Nova Scotia, it is a fact that as late as 1765 Fort Edward still held Acadian prisoners to the number of four hundred. Many of these had been captured in the mountains, islands and other secluded spots where they had taken refuge. They were at last set free, and they, with the returning wanderers, were allowed to take up land and settle. Indeed, their supplanters found that their services would be valuable, as the Acadians knew more about building and maintaining dykes than did the English. The latter sent a memorial to Governor Wilmot stating that " the French Acadians who have hitherto been stationed in this country have been of great use as laborers in

assisting in the carrying on of our business in agricul-
ture and improvement in general, but particularly in
repairing and making dykes, a work which they are
accustomed to and experienced in; and we find that
without their further assistance many of us cannot
continue our improvements, nor plow, nor sow the
lands, nor finish the dyking still required to secure the
lands from the salt water; and being convinced from
experience that unless those dyke lands are enclosed
we cannot with certainty raise bread for our subsistence." The descendants of those who returned are
still found in the villages of St. Mary's, Port Acadia,
Meteghan, Church Point, and other towns in this part
of the peninsula.

When the expatriation took place at Annapolis
many escaped and took refuge in the mountain and
lake region in and about the present city of Yar-
mouth. P. H. Smith, in his " Acadia, A Lost Chapter in American History," thus describes this section
of Nova Scotia: " The scenery of Argyl Bay is
extremely beautiful of its kind,—cottages embowered
in the forests of fir and spruce, and the masts of the
small fishing vessels peeping up from every little
cove, with innumerable islands and peninsulas enclos-
ing the blue sea in every direction; while beyond, and
amid the scenery of the Tusket Lakes, are the blue
mountains, the paradise of moose and trout."

Among these narrow passes hundreds of the
Acadians took refuge during the persecutions of
1755-60, and several settlements were formed by

them here. The remains of a flourishing one existed up to a recent period at the head of Chegogin marsh, and the apple-trees, stone walls and cellars on the Chebogue River are said to be relics of the same people.

But even the solitude and seclusion of this spot did not save them from the pursuit of their enemies. A British frigate was sent down to hunt them out. A small boat was despatched to the mouth of the Tusket River, and, guided by native pilots, ascended the stream and its chain of lakes to invest this asylum. The invaders had advanced to within a mile of the village, and were arrived at a narrow place where the river is twenty to thirty yards in width. Here the pass is overarched by the branches of the somber pine.   An ambuscade had been formed by the fugitives, and the unsuspecting crew, surprised under the very muzzles of their assailants' guns, received a fatal discharge of musketry, which destroyed the entire party.

This sanguinary triumph only served to render the fate of the Acadians more certain, and they were at last compelled to flee. Some escaped to the woods and affiliated with the Indians, never afterward returning to the haunts or the habits of the white man; but the greater part were captured and transported with their families to England.

Thirty years after the expatriation, families, sweethearts and lovers were still striving to be reunited. Advertisements were seen in the then limited number of publications of the country asking for the missing ones, or endeavoring to make known to them that the advertiser was alive.

Along the shores of the Gulf of St. Lawrence, in the northern part of New Brunswick, in the northern part of Maine, and in northern Vermont, may the descendants of the Acadians be found. In 1764 the total number remaining in the Province of Nova Scotia was about fifteen hundred, besides about three hundred on Prince Edward Island. About half of the latter afterwards went to the West Indies, but the climate was unsuited to them, and most of them died.

Between the towns of Dorchester and Moneton, in the beautiful and picturesque valley of theMemram-cook, we find a people bearing unmistakable evidence of Acadian origin. They are the descendants of the French Neutrals, as their dialect and names indicate. The Le Blancs, Melansons, Le Sours and others are among the earliest names found in the records of this people. After the first deportation, many of those who escaped from Lawrence and his soldiery sought refuge in the wilds of New Brunswick. Up the St. John they pushed their way as far as the present city of Fredericton. Here they began to clear the forests and found homes anew. Soon the little settlement of St. Anne began to grow, and for seventeen years or more its inhabitants, who once dwelt by the Basin of Minas, were prosperous, happy and unmolested.

But another calamity was to befall them. Their

persecutions had ceased for years, and apparently the settlers of St. Anne's were far enough away from the scenes of strife and conflict in which the colonists and the mother country were engaged to be perfectly secure. Such was not the case. The Revolution being over, thousands of loyalists of the colonies found themselves fugitives from their homes, exiles as the Acadians had been. In 1784 many of these loyalists found the rich and fertile spot at St. Anne, drove the Acadians out, took possession of their houses and lands, and they again became exiles and wanderers. St. Anne became Fredericton, and again into the depths of the forest primeval plunged the children of Acadia.

In the great forests of northern New Brunswick and northeastern Maine, on the Madawaska and St. John Rivers, they began again to build homes,— homes in which their descendants now rest securely, and from which they can never be driven, except through due process of law. Here for over a century, in almost perfect isolation from the rest of the world, for many years almost unknown to the people of Maine, within whose boundaries many of them had settled, have dwelt the descendants of the exiles who made their way up along the coast from the Carolinas and Virginia.

There still remained after the deportation of 1755, on the River St. John, the Gulf shores, and on Prince Edward Island, some ten thousand Acadians. About fifteen hundred of these went to Quebec by the St.

Lawrence between 1756 and 1758; others to the number of some hundreds ascended the St. John River, in 1759 and 1760, and settled in the district of Three Rivers, where their descendants are to be found to-day. Many of these travelers died before reaching their destination. There remained after these two migrations about eight thousand, of whom at least fifty-five hundred found a refuge on Prince Edward Island. This number was somewhat increased by fugitives from Nova Scotia.

After the capture of Louisbourg by Boscawain, these people, to the number of between three and four thousand, were deported. Some were sent to England, where half of them died from various causes; others were left in France, at St. Malo, Boulogne, and other ports; some were sent to the Island of Jersey; while a part never reached Europe, as the vessels on which they were embarked were unseaworthy, and went to the bottom with all their precious human freight.

Prior to the peace of 1763 the Acadians began to work their way back from the southern colonies, as we have previously seen, to Acadia,—that at least being their objective point. Grand-Pré and the Minas region were already in the possession of English settlers, and as a matter of fact but one body of all those who started from the various places of exile ever reached the peninsula of Acadia or Nova Scotia, and these were the founders of the settlements at Cape Sable and St. Mary's Bay.

As previously stated, this band of the exiles sailed back from South Carolina in two old vessels, and landed at the mouth of the River St. John. From this place they made their way on foot along the shore of the Bay of Fundy, around the Basin of Minas, only to find their lands in the possession of others. They were thus forced again to take up their weary march eastward, and finally found a resting-place on the barren shores of the east end of the peninsula.

The " River St. John," by which name the settlement at its mouth was known in early days, was the oldest of all the Acadian settlements, but by no means the most thriving. Indeed, it was so small and insignificant as to escape for several years the ravages of the English and colonial soldiery. The ancient Seigneurie of Jemseg, or Jemsek, was forty leagues up the river. It had been conceded to the Damour family, who were already settled there in 1686. In 1693 there were twenty-one inhabitants; in 1698, fifty; in 1739, one hundred and sixteen. At the mouth of the St. John some of Charnisay's colonists were found, protected by a small fort; this settlement was broken up at the time of the Acadian dispersion.

To the settlement on the St. John, near Grand Lake, came the fugitives from the various hiding-places in the Northeast, and some from South Carolina; at one time there were between twelve and fourteen hundred Acadians gathered at this place. Food became scarce, and the people were forced

Old Blacksmith Shop on the site of the one used by the Acadians, Grand-Pré.

to migrate. A large number went to Quebec; some continued on up the river to Three Rivers; others became pirates and harassed British commerce. In 1758 those who remained were surprised by a party under Monckton and driven up the river.

The larger part of those who remained in New Brunswick went up the River St. John, and a short distance above the site of Fredericton founded the village of St. Anne. Early in 1759 this village was attacked by some New England Rangers under Hazen; six women and children were killed, twenty-three prisoners were taken, and the village was burned.

Perley, a local historian, states that in 1762 his grandfather, with an exploring party, found the blackened ruins of their buildings. In 1761 Governor Bulkley reported that there were forty Acadians at this place who had not made submission. They were ordered to leave, without even gathering their crops. Again, in 1766, Bulkley ordered the people in the vicinity, except six families, to be chosen by the priest, Father Bailly, to remove.

A letter written by this Father Bailly from Ekouipahan to Bishop Briand, June 20th, 1766, says: "There are eleven Acadian families on the outskirts of the village, the same ones whom your Lordship kindly confirmed at St. Anne. The Acadians who have remained long among the English are still very fervent; their only fault is a great wrongheadedness, either on the subject of remaining each in his own district and being unwilling to unite with the rest, or in the matter of land, which they want to hold under old-time conditions, responsible to the King alone. This is the reproach of the English, who detest them. The Government is not willing to give them land on this condition, yet exacts from them an oath of fidelity. It is a hard task to attend to them, for they live in districts apart from one another;—during the summer on the seashore fishing, and in the winter in the woods hunting."

Until the close of the Revolution New Brunswick had few inhabitants except the Acadians and Indians. The few English in the Province were on the seacoast, and the settlements were small. At the close of the Revolution thousands of Tories left the States with the English troops, and found homes in the various colonies of the North. Lands were given them by the English Government in the Province of New Brunswick, which included land already occupied by the refugee Acadians. The loyalists found the Acadians in possession, but they ordered them to " move on." Casgrain says: " The establishment at the mouth of the St. John became a living hell for the Acadians who held to their lands. Some of them went away to join their dispossessed brethren who had founded the Madawaska colony."

CHAPTER XIX.

The settlement of the valley of the upper St. John, which some authorities have placed as early as 1756, is a matter of uncertainty as to date, the establishment of a colony at Madawaska at that early period being only a matter of Acadian tradition. There is no doubt, however, about the immigration to that point thirty years later, when the loyalists forced them out of the Fredericton region. Twenty families in 1784 made their way up the St. John in boats, carrying their effects around the Grand Falls, and " thirty leagues from any habitation, axe in hand, opened up the plains of Madawaska."

The Acadians found here two Canadians keeping a trading house. These two men were Pierre Lizotte and Pierre Duperre, who had located in this section in 1783. The valley of the upper St. John, while possibly not occupied before Lizotte's time, was known to the French long before. Champlain in 1612 and Francklin in 1686 both indicate it on their maps, the latter applying the word " Madawaska " to Lake Temisquata. The name is from the Indian word Med-a-wes-kek, signifying " porcupine place," the French pronouncing it Madoueska, and the English changing it to its present pronunciation.

There is no doubt that the character of the coun-

try was known to the Acadian exiles before they settled there, and that they did not go into the wilderness in ignorance of where they were finally to settle.
The Acadian hunter and trapper, the Canadian Indians, and the French Canadian of the lower St. Lawrence, were familiar with the country south of the
St. Lawrence for many miles. They knew of the
settlement at St. Anne's, had visited it, and had also
visited those south as far as the mouth of the St. John
River; in fact, this river was the natural highway
between Canada and the coast settlements of the
French.

Madawaska was then a promised land to these
wanderers. Mr. Deane, one of the American Com-
missioners to settle the boundary disputes between
Maine and New Brunswick, and who, with Mr.
Davies, the other Commissioner, traveled through
this region in 1828, says: " The Acadians, or neutral
French, whose ancestors had been settled at the head
of the Bay of Fundy, or in that country now called
Nova Scotia, and had been driven from thence and
had established themselves at St. Anne's, now Fredericton, and in that region, being disturbed by the in-
troduction of the refugees and the acts of the Governor of New Brunswick, which dispossessed them of
their farms, fled up the St. John in search of places of
residence out of the reach of British laws and oppres-
sion. Twenty or more families moved, and settled
themselves on the St. John, below the trading station,
which Pierre Duperre had made a few years before.

Here they continued in unmolested enjoyment of their property for some years."

We may also here quote from Mr. Davies, the other Commissioner: " It may be proper to advert to the situation of a colony of French settlers which planted itself within our territory, principally, if not entirely, since the acknowledgment of and establishment of the bounds of Massachusetts by the treaty of 1783. Situated near the borders of the American territory, they appear to have preserved their neutral character, and to have remained as a people by themselves, so far as they might be permitted by their position toward the Province of New Brunswick. Without having any sympathy with the system established in that government, they have not been in condition to oppose the exercise of any power that might be exerted over them."

In 1792 twenty-four heads of families, acting for thirty-one families, the total number in the settlement, petitioned the Archbishop of Quebec, asking permission to build a church. The petition was drawn up by Father Paquette, for the people themselves could neither read nor write. He indicated in the margin, beside each name, the nationality of the signers, about one-half of whom were Canadian French. The purely Acadian names are descendants of the original families of 1671. The petition was granted, and the church was erected on the north side of the St. John, and dedicated to St. Basil. From Mr. Dean's account we gather something of the life and character of these people, who had not changed much during all the period of their vicissitudes.

" A few families established themselves in 1807 a few miles above the mouth of the Madawaska River. They all lived in mutual good-fellowship, recognizing and practicing the duties of morality and religion, and governed solely by the laws of honor and common-sense. They continued to live in this manner to as late a period as 1818. The British had made no grant higher up the St. John than those mentioned above, unless the transportation of the mail through to Canada and the granting of a commission to Pierre Duperre in 1798 as captain of militia, there being no military organization until twenty-eight years afterwards, may be called acts of jurisdiction. . . . About this time [1790] another body of the descendants of the Acadians, or neutral French, who had sought refuge on the Kennebecasis River, were there disturbed in their possession, and in a like manner sought a refuge with their countrymen at Madawaska. After having resided at Madawaska some years they were induced, as their countrymen had been, to receive from the Governor of New Brunswick grants of the land they had taken into possession."

Mr. Davies says: " Little occasion could be presented for the employment of criminal process among the relics of a primitive population represented as of a mild, industrious, frugal and pious character, desirous of finding a refuge under the patriarchal and spiritual power of religion. It has been the custom for them to settle their civil affairs of every description, including their accidental disputes and differences, by the aid of one or two arbitrators or umpires associated with the Catholic priest, who is commonly a missionary from Canada."

The first American settlement in this extreme northeastern point of Maine was in 1817, and the first knowledge the authorities of Maine seem to have had of the long-existing Acadian settlements was about this time. The American census of 1820 for the district showed a population of over eleven hundred. There are fifty-five distinct family names, and but two of them American or English.

The boundary dispute between Maine and New Brunswick was settled by the treaty of 1843, the line passing through the middle of the St. John River, thus cutting the Madawaska settlement in two. In all the disputes over the boundary the Acadians seem to have been entirely indifferent; they had, of course, received grants from the British authorities of the land which they had long occupied. They could not be induced to take an active part in the efforts of the Americans to form local governing bodies; town meetings, the elixir of New England political life, had no fascination for the peasant of the Madawaska settlement. Like their ancestors of Acadia, they simply desired to be left alone. They had no desire to become an appendage to the American nation; their experience with the people of the adjoining settlements was not such as to invite them to participate in their strenuous life. In fact, the Maine Yankee was too swift and pushing for them. When the dispute was settled, and those south of the St. John became citizens of the United States, they accepted the fact, and proceeded on the even tenor of their way.

Jackson, in his geological report for the year 1836, covers the state of society and education, at that period, and says: " The whole tract between the Madawaska and this line [boundary] is settled by Acadians, and is known under the name of the Madawaska settlement. This district was incorporated as a town by the State of Maine, but difficulties having ensued as to the right of jurisdiction, it was agreed to leave the place in statu quo until the claims of the two countries should be adjusted, an injunction being placed, by mutual agreement, against cutting timber upon the disputed territory. . . . The population of the Madawaska settlement is estimated at three thousand souls, nine hundred of whom live above the Little Falls. Most of the settlers are descendants of the French neutrals, who were driven by British violence from their homes in Nova Scotia. These people first established themselves above Fredericton, and subsequently removed above the Grand Falls and effected a settlement. The Acadians are a very peculiar people, remarkable for the simplicity of their manners and their fidelity to their employers. Although they are said to be ' sharp at a bargain,' they are remarkably honest, industrious and respectful, and are polite and hospitable to each other and to strangers.

" It is curious to observe how perfectly they have retained all their French peculiarities. The forms of their houses, the decorations of their apartments, their dress, modes of cookery, etc., are exactly as they were originally in the land of their ancestors. They speak a kind of *patois*, or corrupted French, but perfectly understand the modern language as spoken in Paris. But few persons can be found who understand or speak English, and these are such as from the necessities of trade have learned a few words of the language. None of the women or children either understand or speak English. The Acadians are a cheerful, contented and happy people, social in their intercourse, and they never pass each other without a kind salutation. While they thus retain all the marked characteristics of the French peasantry, it is curious that they appear to know but little respecting the country from which they originated, and but few of them have the least idea of its geographical situation. Thus we were asked, when we spoke of France, if it were not separated from England by a river, or if it was near the coast of Nova Scotia; and one of them inquired if Bethlehem, where Christ was born, was not a town in France? Since they have no schools, and their knowledge is but traditional, it is not surprising that they should remain ignorant of geography and history. I can account for their

9

understanding the pure French language by the circumstance that they are supplied with Catholic priests from the mother country, who, of course, speak to them in that tongue. Those who visit Madawaska must remember that no money passes current there but silver, for the people do not know how to read, and will not take bank-notes, for they have often been imposed upon, since they are unable to distinguish between a five-dollar, a five-pound and a five-shilling note. As there are no taverns in this settlement every family the traveler calls on will furnish accommodations, for which they expect a reasonable compensation; and he will always be sure of kind treatment, which is beyond price. I have been thus particular in speaking of the Acadian settlers of Madawaska, because little is generally known of their manners or customs, many people having the idea that they are semi-savages, because, like the aboriginal inhabitants, they live principally by hunting."

In 1843, the year of the Ashburton treaty, which settled the boundary dispute, some of the inhabitants of this section, Americans beyond all doubt, wrote thus to Governor Kavanagh: "It is well known to you that the settlements on the American side of the St. John extend on the margin of the river continuously from Fort Kent to the easterly line of the State, a distance of nearly sixty miles, and from the same point westwardly, with some interruptions, to Little Black River, at its intersection with the St. John, a distance of thirty miles more. The whole settlement is separated from the other settlements of the State of Maine by an unbroken forest of from thirty to sixty miles in breadth. It is composed of Acadian and Canadian French, a few Irishmen and provincial Englishmen, and here and there an American. The people are generally unacquainted with our laws and customs, unable to read or write, and but few understand our language. Their business intercourse has been wholly with New Brunswick and Canada. They have lived under British laws, and are too ignorant to be at present capable of self-government."

Rev. Charles W. Collins, Chancellor of the Roman Catholic Diocese of Portland, Maine, sums up the Acadian situation so far as Madawaska and its settlements are concerned, in the following language: " If an indictment is to be formulated against the social and educational backwardness of this part of the State, in justice it ought not to retroact beyond 1850. During the past half century the progress of Madawaska has been steady, conservative and (considering the many obstacles) creditable to its people. This knot of settlements is situated in the extreme north, three hundred miles from the seaboard, totally removed from American railroads, in a remote part of a relatively unprosperous State. It has had the further disadvantage of being cut in twain and half-allotted to Canada. Racially and territorially it is to-day more Canadian than American, yet for internal improvements it has had to look to a common-

wealth unable to help it much. It is almost exclusively a farming country; its main source of income
is the sale of agricultural products. The soil, though
fertile, is by no means to be compared with that of
Nova Scotia or the great Aroostook valley. In order
to sell his products the Madawaska farmer has been
compelled to convey them long miles by wagon, or
dispose of them at a ruinous rate to itinerant traders.
The agricultural development of other parts of the
State has worked him nothing but harm. The land
itself has been overworked, and fertilizers are beyond
his purse. In bad years he has been driven to the
money-lender, and this temporary expedient, as
always, has become a widely-prevailing condition,
sapping industry and driving off the energetic.
Scores, nay hundreds, of these farms are loaded with
the mortgage incubus, and held in precarious tenure.
This state of things, though it has not resulted in
starvation, has held the settlers in an ever-tightening
grip of poverty. The increase of population, also,
has its disadvantages. The people of the younger
generation have taken up new concessions in the
interior, only to repeat the sorrowful experience of
their fathers.

" Lumbering has, at certain seasons of the year,
given employment to a number of the inhabitants,
but has worked great harm to the farming industry.
All manufactured goods are luxuries, on account of
the cost of carriage. Across the river is a community
almost in the same condition. Moreover, the Acadian

has not the American energy and progressiveness, but even if he had, we could not argue much more for him than has been the result in the rural districts in other parts of the State. In spite of obstacles the most discouraging, the Madawaska country during the past fifty years has accomplished much. There are now in the district commonly called Madawaska, which includes all the country between Van Buren and Saint Francis, and some considerable inland settlements, nine churches, eight of these with resident clergymen, who also attend many missions without churches. There is a college at Van Buren, conducted by the Marist fathers, with a corps of nine professors and one hundred students. In three places—Van Buren, Frenchville and Wallagras—are religious schools under charge of Good Shepherd, Rosary and Franciscan Sisters."

CHAPTER XX.

The Acadians who went from Philadelphia to Louisiana settled on the Bayou Teche. " West of this stream," says Cable, " lies a beautiful undulating prairie, some thirty-nine hundred square miles in extent, dotted with artificial homestead groves, with fields of sugar-cane, cotton and corn, and with herds of ponies and keen horned cattle feeding on its short, nutritious turf. Their herdsmen speak an ancient patois, and have the blue eyes and light brown hair of northern France. But not yet have we found the Creoles. The Creoles smile and sometimes even frown at these : these are the children of those famed Nova Scotian exiles whose banishment from their homes by the British in arms in 1755 has so often been celebrated in romance; they still bear the name of Acadians. They are found not only on the western side of the Teche, but in all this French-speaking region of Louisiana. But these vast prairies of Attakapas and Opelousas are peculiarly theirs, and here they largely outnumber that haughtier Louisianian who endeavors to withhold as well from him as from the American the proud appellation of Creole."

" Their [the Acadians'] descendants," says Alcée Fortier, " are to be found in every parish of lower Louisiana. They form an important and useful part

of our population. Although a simple farming people, they have had some men of eminence in the
State, and their lot has been by no means miserable."
Judge Joseph A. Breaux, of the Supreme Court of
Louisiana, who is very much interested in the Acadians, in a letter to the author, remarks that " the
Acadians in the South have not entirely preserved
the simplicity which marked the original Acadian and
his descendants in the Northeast. The varied con-
tacts have, to some extent, lost him his identity as an
Acadian. He is loyal as a citizen, and usually a fairly
good neighbor. Many of them are poor, and our
school system, efficient enough in the cities, is wanting in the country. The young men (nearly all)
speak the English, and know very little of the Acadians. They (many of them) avoid all reference to
Acadians, and would be pleased to be known exclusively as Americans, forgetting that the good citizenship of our country is made up of the best elements
of all nationalities."

It is not to be understood that all the Acadians of
Louisiana are the descendants of those who left Philadelphia in 1757. It is possible that many of the
exiles sent to Georgia and the Carolinas reached
Louisiana in 1756, and possibly in the latter part of
1755. Here as elsewhere they seem to have preserved few if any actual records of their migration,
and they have largely lost all interest in the romantic
but sad history of their ancestors. They seem to be
devoid of interest in their traditional history, or loth

to disclose it to strangers. Only in the Madawaska region of Maine and New Brunswick, at St. Mary's Bay and the surrounding settlements in Nova Scotia, and in the Acadian settlements of Louisiana, has the descendant of the exiles alone preserved his identity. In these widely-separated districts, while the contact has been different, he has clung to his mother tongue with all the tenacity of the Pennsylvania German, who, in the midst of an English-speaking people for nearly two centuries, still in his home uses his " mutter spreche."

For years these remnants of the exiles were prac- tically isolated from all influences which lead to the amalgamation of distinct races, and as a matter of fact there is as yet very little mixed blood among them. In Louisiana, while the exiles were well receive by their countrymen, there was yet no dispo- sition on the part of the wealthy and aristocratic planter to more than tolerate his less fortunate brother. The Creole, proud, indolent, pleasure-lov- ing, and withal dominant and domineering, looked upon the Acadians as inferiors, and rarely if ever intermarried with them. The American element, which appeared many years after the Acadian, and was of that doubtful character which may be called a cross between a riverman and a buccaneer, was not at all congenial to the simple peasantry of the Aca- dian settlements. These circumstances preserved the purity of the Acadian blood in the South, while in southeastern Nova Scotia race and religious feeling and prejudices have, with few exceptions, kept the strain pure.

In the Madawaska district, whatever of mixture there is comes through intermarriage with French Canadians. Those who went to Canada, and they compose the great majority of those who remained on the American continent, became swallowed up in the great mass of the French population and lost their identity entirely. It has been isolation only which has preserved to any body of these people their distinctive appellation of "Acadian," and only in Louisiana are their descendants known by the name, and there more commonly "Cadian" or "Cajan."

CHAPTER XXI.

Not the least interesting feature in the story of
Evangeline and her people is that of the original of
the character. However much the exigencies of
poetry may have caused a divergence from the facts
in producing a harmonious whole, the tradition preserved in one of the exile families, of the wanderings
and the peculiarly sad fate of a young Acadian girl,
evidently forms the basis of Longfellow's poem.

The Mouton family of Louisiana, descended from
the Acadian exiles, has long preserved as part of its
family inheritance the sad story of Emmeline Labiche, the original Evangeline.

Senator Mouton, of Louisiana, who was a personal
friend of Longfellow, gave to the poet the story of
the young girl who was adopted into his family in
the village of St. Gabriel in the old Acadian days, and
after the dispersion, and in all their wanderings,
found her home with the family in its exile. It is
told in the words of an ancestor who was among
those deported, and is substantially as follows :

" Emmeline Labiche was an orphan girl of Acadia,
whose parents died when she was yet a child, and who
was taken into our family and adopted.

" She was sweet-tempered and loving, and grew to
womanhood with all the attractions of her sex. Al-

though not a beauty in the sense usually given to the word, she was looked upon as the handsomest girl in St. Gabriel. . . . Emmeline had just completed her sixteenth year, and was on the eve of marrying a deserving, laborious and well-to-do man of St. Gabriel, named Louis Arsenaux. Their mutual love dated back to their earliest years, and was concealed from no one. . . . Their banns had been published in the village church, the nuptial day was fixed . . . when the barbarous scatterment of our colony took place. Our oppressors had driven us toward the seashore where their ships rode at anchor, and Louis, resisting with rage and despair, was wounded by them.

" Emmeline witnessed the whole scene. . . . Tearless and speechless she stood fixed to the spot. When the white sails vanished in the distance . . . she clasped me in her arms and in an agony of grief sobbed piteously. By degrees the violence of her grief subsided, but the sadness of her countenance betokened the sorrow that preyed upon her heart.

" Henceforward she lived a quiet and retired life, mingling no more with her companions, and taking no part in their amusements. The remembrance of her lost love remained enshrined in her heart.

" Thus she lived in our midst, always sweet-tempered, with such sadness depicted on her countenance and with smiles so sorrowful that we had come to look on her not as of this earth, but rather as our guardian angel. Thus it was that we called her no longer Emmeline, but ' Evangeline,' or ' God's little angel.' . . .

" Emmeline had been exiled to Maryland with us. She followed me in my long overland journey from Maryland to Louisiana.

"When we reached the Teche country at the Poste de Attakapas we found the whole population congregated to welcome us. When we landed from the boat Emmeline walked by my side. . . . Suddenly, as if fascinated by a vision, she stopped, and then, the silvery tones of her voice vibrating with joy, she cried: ' Mother! mother! it is he. It is Louis !' and she pointed to the tall figure of a man standing beneath an oak. It was Louis Arsenaux. . . . She flew to his side, crying out in an ecstasy of joy and love. He turned ashy pale, and hung his head without uttering a word. ' Louis,' she said, ' why do you turn your eyes away? I am still your Emmeline, your betrothed !'

" With quivering lips and trembling voice he answered: ' Emmeline, do not speak so kindly to me. I am unworthy of you. I can love you no longer. I have pledged my faith to another. Tear from your heart the remembrance of the past and forgive me.' Then he wheeled away and disappeared in the forest.

" A pallor overspread her countenance, and her eyes assumed a vacant stare. . . .

" She followed me like a child without resistance. I clasped her in my arms and wept bitterly. ' Emmeline, my dear, be comforted. There may yet be happiness in store for you.' ' Emmeline, Emmeline,' she muttered to herself, as if to recall that name, and then: ' Who are you ? ' She turned away, her mind unhinged. . . .

" Emmeline never recovered her reason, and a deep melancholy ever possessed her. Her beautiful countenance was lighted by a sad smile which made her all the fairer. She never recognized any one but me, and nestling in my arms . . . would bestow on me the most endearing names. She spoke of Acadia and Louis in such terms that one could not listen to her without shedding tears. She fancied herself still the sweet girl of sixteen on the eve of marrying her chosen one, whom she loved with so much devotion and constancy. . . . Sinking at last under the ravages of her mental disease she expired in my arms."

Such is the story of Emmeline Labiche, as told to Longfellow by Governor, afterwards Senator, Alexander Mouton, of Louisiana, and as handed down in the records and traditions of the Mouton family, in which the young girl found home, shelter and loving-kindness.

APPENDIX.

APPENDIX

LETTER FROM HON. C. H. MOUTON.

Lafayette, June 7th, A.D. 1903.

DR. GEORGE P. BIBLE.

Dear Sir: Your kind and courteous letter of the 20th of April was appreciably received and considered. Sickness in my family is cause of the delay for not having answered sooner. I am glad to be able to give you some information concerning the Acadian exiles who have settled in the prairies between the Bayou (River) Teyche (now written Têche) and the River Mermento, in southwestern Louisiana. Among their numerous descendants, I know the Benoît, Blanchard, Boutin, Bourgue, Boudro, who write their name " Boudreau," Brasseux, Breaux, Comeau, Douarou, Doucet, Dugas, Dupuy or Dupuis, Gautereau, Girouard, Grangé, Hebert, the *Broussard*, Landry, Leblanc, Lejeune, Martin, Melanson (who write their name Melançon), the Mouton, the Richard, Roy, Teriau (written here, Thériot), Thibodeaux, Trahan, Vincent. The name of Broussard is not on the list, kindly enclosed in your letter.

In answer to your question I will state that my grandfather, Jean (John) Mouton, was born at Port Royal, Acadia, about the year 1753 or 1754; his father's name was Salvator Mouton, an Acadian exile, who came to Louisiana and settled on the Mississippi River, in what is called St. Charles parish, a few miles above New Orleans, in what year I cannot state, but by family tradition I know that my grandfather was a young boy (as we Acadians say, " Un petit garçon ") when his father came to Louisiana. When old Salvator Mouton died my grandfather was a minor. When a man he came to

10

St. Martin parish, on the river Teyche, near the Evangeline Oak of Longfellow, and there met an old Acadian exile woman, widow of Antoine Borda, and he there married a daughter of said widow Borda.

After his marriage, Widow Borda came and lived with grandfather, and died at the age of one hundred and four years.

The widow Borda, whose family name was Martin, was a widow Robichaud, at the time she was exiled from Acadia; she had two children (girls). How and when she reached the parish of St. Martin, I cannot say; but after she got to St. Martin (then the county of Attakapas) she contracted a second marriage with Dr. Antoine Borda, a Frenchman, and there my grandfather met the family and married. I know by family tradition that old Mrs. Borda, my great-grandmother, was very poor and destitute when she reached St. Martin, on the River Têche. Herewith I send a sketch or diagram of the wooden box, in which she carried her clothes and her children's, when they came from Acadia to Louisiana, which said wooden box is kept by our family as an heirloom.

I will be eighty years old next December, and as you can see I write with difficulty, but if you desire more information on this subject, if I can give it, I will do so with pleasure.

I am, sir, respectfully yours,

C. H. MOUTON.

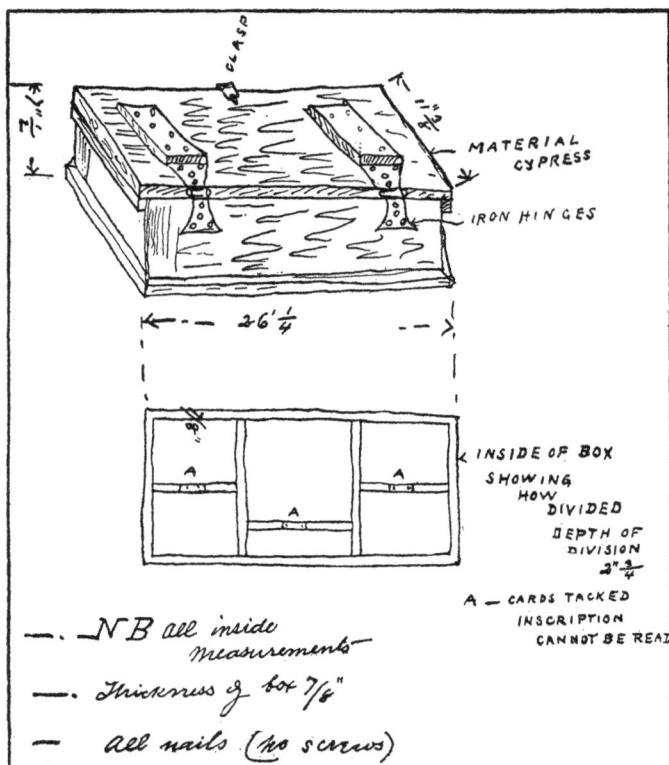

Clasp

7/8"

MATERIAL
CYPRESS

IRON HINGES

26' 1/4

INSIDE OF BOX

SHOWING
HOW
DIVIDED

DEPTH OF
DIVISION

2" 3/4

A — CARDS TACKED
INSCRIPTION
CANNOT BE READ

—. N B all inside
measurements

—. Thickness of box 7/8"

— all nails (no screws)

WOODEN CHEST BELONGING TO AN ACADIAN EXILE.

New Orleans, March 25th, 1903.

MR. GEORGE P. BIBLE,
           Philadelphia, Pa.

Dear Sir: Yesterday I received your letter dated the 20th inst.

In answer to your inquiry, I will state that I have always understood that nearly all the Acadians who came to Louisiana came first to Georgia and North Carolina, and afterward to Louisiana, settling on the Mississippi River, near Baton Rouge. Others came afterward and found their way to the Acadian Coast on the Mississippi, and others went to the interior on the Tèche River, of the Attakapas, and in the prairies of Opelousas.

A singular phase followed the expulsion; not many years had passed, when the Acadians that had returned to Nova Scotia and New Brunswick, as well as Prince Edward Island, joined the English in defending the Canadian Territory and in opposing the American colonists. While down here, the Acadian sympathized with the colonists and a number became soldiers of Galvez, who was the Spanish Governor of the Colony of Louisiana, and opposed the English, and fought them at several places.

I am confident that the Acadians did not all come by way of Georgia and North Carolina, nor do I believe that they all came about the same time. It is probable that a few families came at first and others in course of time followed. They in time, as you doubtless are aware, became good citizens of the United States of America.

If you wish any particular information regarding the

Acadians, let me know. It will afford me pleasure to attend to any request you may deem proper to make.

Sincerely yours,

JOSEPH A. BREAUX.

New Orleans, April 10th, 1903.

DR. GEORGE P. BIBLE,

Temple Building, Phila., Penna.

Dear Sir: I must say that the Acadians in the South have not entirely preserved the simplicity which marked the original Acadian and his descendants in the Northeast. The varied contracts have to some extent lost him his identity as an Acadian.

He is loyal as a citizen and usually a fairly good neighbor.

Many of them are poor, and our school system, efficient enough in cities, is wanting in the country.

The young men (nearly all) speak the English, and know very little of the Acadians. They (many of them) avoid all reference to Acadians, and would be pleased to be known exclusively as Americans, forgetting that the good citizenship of our country is made up of the best elements of all nationalities.

I send you a copy of the *Times-Democrat*. On the 12th page you will find an incident prettily told of Desire LeBlanc, of Vermillion, a descendant of an Acadian. It may interest you.

By the way, I understand that the LeBlancs, after the expulsion, came here by way of Philadelphia (where they remained a few years), and one of them became influential in your city.

Sincerely yours,

JOSEPH A. BREAUX.

The following sketch from the New Orleans *Times-Democrat,* told simply and beautifully, will give one an insight into a phase of character of at least one modern Acadian, who has not degenerated from the simplicity of his fathers or the un-ostentatious charity, which anticipates the wants, and gives before being asked:

SIMPLE "CAJAN" A SAMARITAN TO ALL HIS POOR NEIGHBORS.

DESIRE LE BLANC TAKES PLEASURE IN BRINGING THE AFFLICTED OF INDIAN BAYOU TO CHARITY HOSPITAL FOR TREATMENT.

At daylight yesterday morning a reporter of the *Times-Democrat* saw a man sneaking out of the building at 1318 Canal Street. As the man got to the corner he hesitated as if undecided what street he would take. Presently he turned in the direction of the Charity Hospital, the reporter following. Two blocks away the man was halted and asked the time. The stranger pulled out his watch, gave the desired information, and in the next breath invited the reporter to join him in a drink. Instead of shadowing "a dangerous and suspicious character," below is a short account of one of the most re-markable characters in this or any other State.

Desire LeBlanc is a "Creole" living at Indian Bayou, Ver-million parish. He was born near his present home, is mar-ried and has six children. In the Catholic Cemetery, near Indian Bayou, are six graves, where lie the bodies of six other children. Mr. LeBlanc owns a little rice farm. In this field he has toiled for thirty years, sometimes harvesting good crops and in other years meeting with total failure. But he has saved a few dollars, owes no man money or ill-will, and in all that country there is none so honored and loved as this simple, uneducated and grizzled " Cajan." Ten years ago he visited New Orleans for the first time. He had heard of the big Charity Hospital, and he wanted to see it. Ten days later he came again, this time bringing his wife, then an invalid. She was in the hospital for two months, and was discharged as cured. Returning home, Mr. LeBlanc found one of his children ill, and back he came with another patient. And so on, he has been making trips to New Orleans on an average of twice a month for all these years, each time bringing some one of his neighbors needing medical attention. He speaks English brokenly.

"I pay their expenses, too," he told the reporter. " Of course, there is no charge at the hospital, but pay the railroad fares. Few of my neighbors are financially able to make even so short a trip. Even if they were, would not permit them to pay. It is my chief pleasure in life—such acts as these and the love of my family. I have brought men, women and children here in all sorts of conditions. Not long ago I came with a little boy whose eyes had been eaten out by smallpox. He would have died in another day. His eyesight is gone, but otherwise he is well.

" Who did I bring this time? Adon Boullet, aged three years. On Monday, while I was plowing, the word came that the little fellow had swallowed some grains of corn and that one of these had lodged in his windpipe. Before I reached the Boullet home the grain had been dislodged, but the child was seized with convulsions. When the next train passed I was on board with the boy. The doctors at the hospital say there is no further danger. But I must go to see him before I leave. I would stay for another day, but you see some one else might get sick at Indian Bayou, and they would cry, 'Where is Desire LeBlanc ?'

" How much money and time these trips have cost? Oh, I

do not keep account of such trifles. The time is nothing, and the money? Ah! I have enough always to buy wine for the wife, books for the children and pay for the church. And those children—you must come to see them sometime—three girls and three boys, the finest children in the world. I can not read or write, but they read for me and write to New Orleans for me when some of my friends here are sick.

"Come to Indian Bayou," he said, "and ask the first person you meet where Desire LeBlanc lives, and while he is directing you to my home he will tell you that I am the happiest man in the parish."

At sunrise Mr. LeBlanc was at the hospital inquiring as to the condition of Adon Boullet. At eight o'clock he took a train for Indian Bayou, where, he said, his wife and six children would be at the depot to meet him.

And this is the man the reporter took for a thief. He came tiptoeing out of the boarding house because he did not wish to awaken the other guests.

STATISTICS OF THE DEPORTATION.

Colonel Winslow, under whose supervision the deportation from the Minas district was made, gives the following summary of persons deported:

Males, from ten years	446	
Deputies, prisoners at Halifax	37	
Men	——	483
Women, married	337	
Sons	527	
Daughters	576	
		——1,440
Old and infirm, not mentioned	820	

2,743

The following is the list of villages and the number of in-habitants of each, as made by Winslow. The villages are, in most instances, family names. The list shows a difference in numbers between his general summary and the total in the villages, but this is accounted for by the fact that isolated families were taken and not assigned to any village.

NORTH OF MINAS OR CORNWALLIS RIVER.

Villages.	No. of Inhabitants.
De Landry	39
Claude Terriau	41
Des Landry	4
Granger	44
Jean Terriau	65
Comeau	74
Michel	27
Aucoine	77
Trahan	38
Poirier	20
Saulnier	32
Brun	64
Dupuis	65
Hebert	19
Francois	3
Pinons	7
Antoine	51
Claude	80
Herbert Co Ero	74
Claud Landry	74
Navie	3

SOUTH OF MINAS OR CORNWALLIS RIVER.

Jean Le Blanc	30
Pierre Le Blanc	60
Grand Le Blanc	42
Richar	49
Pinour	2

Villages.	No. of Inhabitants.
GASPEREAU.	
Melanson	52
Michel	57
ABOUT GRAND-PRÉ.	
De Pitit (Gotro)	94
(OMITTED) CANARD.	
Landry	15
CANARD.	
Comeau	4
Granger	4
Pinue	3
Hebert	5
La Coste	2
GRAND-PRÉ.	
Grand-Pré	20
GASPEREAU.	
Gaspereau	41

All the names except those in italics are the names of individuals or families. . . . The principal villages on the south side of Minas River, now the Cornwallis, sometimes called Minas or Grand-Pré, were Gotro, Pierre Le Blanc, Michel, Melanson, Grand Le Blanc, Gaspereau, Jean Le Blanc and Grand-Pré. On the north side of the same river, the villages of the Canard section, sometimes called Habitant and Canard, because the settlements were mainly on the Habitant and Canard Rivers, were named: Claude Landry, Antoine, Hebert, Dupuis, Brun, Trahan, Saulnier, Poirier and Hebert. The remaining villages had less than twenty inhabitants.

At Grand-Pré and Gaspereau and along the south side of Minas the common names of the Acadians in the order of their

frequency were: Le Blanc, Melanson, Hebert, Richard. On the
north side the common names were Boudro, Comeau, Landry,
Aucoine, Granger, Terriau, Dupuis. The name Melanson, so
common among the Acadians to-day, was no doubt of Scotch
origin, and belonged to one of Sir William Alexander's
colonists who came to Acadia about 1638. The larger number
of the settlers who became the progenitors of the thousands of
Acadians now living in the maritime provinces [and this is true
of the Acadian of Louisiana] came out from Rochelle, Sain-
tonge and Poiteau, on the west coast of France, between 1633
and 1638. . . . In 1671, when the first census of Acadia was
taken of which we have any record, there were seventy-five
families, made up of four hundred and forty persons. In 1686
Minas had been settled about fifteen years, and had a population of fifty-seven persons. In 1714, the people numbered
eight hundred and seventy-eight. In 1755 there were at least
ten thousand Acadians in Minas. The following is a list of
names at Minas at the time of the deportation: Alin, Aucoine,
Apigne, Boudro, Blanchard, Bourg, Belmere, Brun, Babin, Bras-
sin, Brane, Bugeant, Benois, Bouns, Belfontaine, Bouer, Braux,
Brassaux, Commeau, Capierre, Celestin, Celve, Daigre, Diron,
Dour, Duzoy, David, Dins, Dupuy, Duon, Dupiers, Doulet,
Dusour, Doucet, Lapierre, Leuron, Le Blanc, Le Clane, Le Blun,
Lebar, Leprince, Labous, Lesour, Landry, Michel, Massier,
Munier, Mengean, Richard, Rour, Sosonier, Sorer, Sapin, Sonier,
Semer, Terriot, Trauhase, Tibodo, Tunour, Trahan, Tilhard,
Vinson.

ACADIANS PAYING QUIT-RENTS, 1743—1752-3.

The following Acadians were between the years 1743-1752-3 paying quit rents. These names or a majority of them, are found in the preceding list, but appear there in their original French orthography. We give them here for the purpose of fixing the locations of the several families at these periods. It may be a matter of interest to their descendants, and an aid in tracing certain family genealogy.

QUIT-RENTS PAID BY THE ACADIANS.

1743-1752-3.

	£	s.	d.
Le Blanc and family under Grand-Pré			
Glaude Peters, for Chas. Landree, dec'sd		12	0
Chas. Bourg.			
Noah Mulsel.			
Louis Lange, at Pré, for his own family	2	4	0
1743-54, Eusanne Terriot, for his own family	2	0	0

N.B.—Above was from ye Cobequid inhabitants.

Place.	Date and year.	In whose name given.	Family.	Time.	Sum paid. £ s. d.		
Grand-Pré	11 Feb. 1753 11 Feb. 1754	Jos. Robichau	Chas. Le Blanc	1 yr.	1	0	0
" "	22 Jan. 1753 22 Jan. 1754	M. Gouthers vief Glode Gothers			1	8	0
" "	9 Dec. 1752 9 Dec. 1753	Mishel Le Blanc	Jos. Le Blanc		1	0	0
River Canard	29 Nov. 1752 29 Nov. 1753	Jno. Trahan	Jno. Trahan		2	8	0

Place.	Date and year.	In whose name given.	Family.	Time.	Sum paid. £ s. d.
River Canard	8 Dec.	Loney Liriot	Glaude Liriot		2 1 ½
" "	3	Rene Oquine	Pere Oquine		3 0 0
" "		Jean Comoe	Jno. Comoe		4 0 0
" "		Alume Hebert			2 6 0
" "		Jno. Boudrot	Glaude Boudrot		1 8 0
" "		Jos. Boudrot			0 3 0

Account of quit-rents paid to Cap. Matthew Flower by the inhabitants of Minas and the River Canard in the year 1754:

Place.		In whose name given.		Time.	Sum paid.
Canard		Claude Granger		3 Livre,	2½ Louis
"		Jean Dupuey		2 Livre,	10 Louis
"		Jos. Vincut		2 Livre	
"		C. Hebert		4 Livre	
Minas		John Le Blanc		2 Livre	10 Louis
"		John Doucette		4 Livre	

					£ s. d.
Dele Cote and Rivre		Peir Landrie	Pierre Landrie		3 4 0
"		M. Gauthro	Glaude Landry	1 yr.	1 4 0
"		Augustin Hebain	Jno. Hebain	1 yr.	1 8 0
"		From Lebanc		5 yrs.	10 0 0
"		" Landree		1 yr.	1 0 0
"		" Simon Le Blanc		1 yr.	1 0 0

Canard for the year 1754:

Family name.	When paid.	By whom.	Amount.	Inclusive per annum.
Rene Landry	Feb. 13, 1755	Pre Melanson,	1 3 4	3 4
Rene Grange		Oliver Daigre	1 2 1	2 1
Jean Dupuis		Honore Daigre	1 2 0	1 0
Etienne Hebert		Pre Hebert	1 2 6	2 6
Claude Teriot		J. Bte. Daigre	1 2 4½	2 0 4½
Pierre Anncoin		Pre. Anncoine	1 3 0	3 0
Jean Como		Etienne Como	1 4 0	4 0
For the land occupied by				
Ante Landry,				
Ante Dupuy,		Simon Grange	0 14 0	9 4
Simon Grange,				
In the Baye des Rimbaud.				
Jean Trahan		Pre. Trahan	1 2 8	2 8

LIST OF ORIGINAL GRANTEES OF LAND FROM THE
GOVERNOR OF NEW BRUNSWICK.

The following is a list of the original grantees of land from
the Governor of New Brunswick, and includes families on both
sides of the St. John's River. The list is taken from " Notes
on Madawaska," by Rev. W. O. Raymond:

" The grantees of Acadian origin were Louis Mercure,
Michel Mercure, Joseph Mercure, Alexis Cyr, Oliver Cyr, Marie
Marguerite Daigle, Jean Baptiste Daigle, Paul Cyr, Pierre Cyr,
Alexander Cyr, Jean Baptiste Thibedeau, Jr., Joseph Thibedeau,
Etienne Thibedeau. The grantees of Acadian origin on the
American side of the river were Simon Hebert, Paul Potier,
John Baptiste Cyr, Jr., François Cyr, Jr., Joseph Daigle, Sr.,
Joseph Daigle, Jr., Jaques Cyr, François Cyr, Firmin Cyr, Sr.,
Jean Baptiste Cyr., Jr., Michael Cyr, Joseph Hebert, Antoine
Cyr, Jean Martin, Joseph Cyr, Jr., Jean Baptiste Cyr, Sr., Fir-
min Cyr, Jr., Jean Thibedeau, Sr., Joseph Mezerolle. In addi-
tion to these there are several grantees, whose descendants
claim to be of Acadian origin, and say their ancestors came
from the lower country (pays-bas); but I am not able to de-
termine whether the following are undoubtedly of Acadian
origin or not, viz.: Louis Saufacon, Mathurin Beaulieu, Joseph
Ayotte, Zacharie Ayotte, Alexander Ayotte.

" The second grant, made in the year 1794, extended from
Green River (with many vacancies) to a little below Grand
River. The six names that occur in the former grant are
omitted from the enumeration that follows. Several of the
settlers in this grant are known to have lived at French vil-
lage, on the Kennebecassis. The names of those Acadians who
settled on the east side of the St. John are as follows: Oliver
Thibedeau, Baptiste Thibedeau, Joseph Theriault, Joseph
Theriault, Jr., Oliver Thibedeau, Jr., Jean Thibedeau, Firmin
Thibedeau, Hilarion Cyr. . . . Those Acadians who settled on
the American side are as follows: Gregoire Thibedeau, Louis
La Blanc, Pierre Cormier, Alexis Cormier, Baptiste Cormier,
François Cormier, Joseph Cyr., Jr., Firmin Cyr, Joseph Cyr,
François Violette, Sr., and Augustin Violette."

EVANGELINE

A Tale of Acadie

HENRY WADSWORTH LONGFELLOW

EVANGELINE

A TALE OF ACADIE

This is the forest primeval. The murmuring pines and the hemlocks,
Bearded with moss, and in garments green, indistinct in the twilight,
Stand like Druids of eld, with voices sad and prophetic,
Stand like harpers hoar, with beards that rest on their bosoms.
Loud from its rocky caverns, the deep-voiced neighboring ocean
Speaks, and in accents disconsolate answers the wail of the forest.

This is the forest primeval; but where are the hearts that beneath it
Leaped like the roe, when he hears in the woodland the voice of the
       huntsman?
Where is the thatch-roofed village, the home of Acadian farmers,—
Men whose lives glided on like rivers that water the woodlands,
Darkened by shadows of earth, but reflecting an image of heaven?
Waste are those pleasant farms, and the farmers forever departed!
Scattered like dust and leaves, when the mighty blasts of October
Seize them, and whirl them aloft, and sprinkle them far o'er the ocean.
Naught but tradition remains of the beautiful village of Grand-Pré.

Ye who believe in affection that hopes, and endures, and is patient,
Ye who believe in the beauty and strength of woman's devotion,
List to the mournful tradition still sung by the pines of the forest;
List to a Tale of Love in Acadie, home of the happy.

PART THE FIRST.

I.

In the Acadian land, on the shores of the Basin of Minas,
Distant, secluded, still, the little village of Grand-Pré
Lay in the fruitful valley. Vast meadows stretched to the eastward,
Giving the village its name, and pasture to flocks without number.
Dikes, that the hands of the farmers had raised with labor incessant,
Shut out the turbulent tides; but at stated seasons the flood-gates
Opened, and welcomed the sea to wander at will o'er the meadows.
West and south there were fields of flax, and orchards and cornfields
Spreading afar and unfenced o'er the plain; and away to the north-
         ward
Blomidon rose, and the forests old, and aloft on the mountains
Sea-fogs pitched their tents, and mists from the mighty Atlantic
Looked on the happy valley, but ne'er from their station descended.
There, in the midst of its farms, reposed the Acadian village.
Strongly built were the houses, with frames of oak and of hemlock,
Such as the peasants of Normandy built in the reign of the Henries.
Thatched were the roofs, with dormer-windows; and gables projecting
Over the basement below protected and shaded the doorway.
There in the tranquil evenings of summer, when brightly the sunset
Lighted the village street, and gilded the vanes on the chimneys,
Matrons and maidens sat in snow-white caps and in kirtles
Scarlet and blue and green, with distaffs spinning the golden
Flax for the gossiping looms, whose noisy shuttles within doors
Mingled their sound with the whir of the wheels and the songs of the
         maidens.
Solemnly down the street came the parish priest, and the children
Paused in their play to kiss the hand he extended to bless them.
Reverend walked he among them; and up rose matrons and maidens,
Hailing his slow approach with words of affectionate welcome.
Then came the laborers home from the field, and serenely the sun sank
Down to his rest, and twilight prevailed. Anon from the belfry
Softly the Angelus sounded, and over the roofs of the village
Columns of pale blue smoke, like clouds of incense ascending,
Rose from a hundred hearths, the homes of peace and contentment.
Thus dwelt together in love these simple Acadian farmers,—

Dwelt in the love of God and of man. Alike were they free from
Fear, that reigns with the tyrant, and envy, the vice of republics.
Neither locks had they to their doors, nor bars to their windows;
But their dwellings were open as day and the hearts of the owners;
There the richest was poor, and the poorest lived in abundance.

   Somewhat apart from the village, and nearer the Basin of Minas,
Benedict Bellefontaine, the wealthiest farmer of Grand-Pré,
Dwelt on his goodly acres; and with him, directing the household,
Gentle Evangeline lived, his child, and the pride of the village.
Stalworth and stately in form was the man of seventy winters;
Hearty and hale was he, an oak that is covered with snow-flakes;
White as the snow were his locks, and his cheeks as brown as the
        oak-leaves.
Fair was she to behold, that maiden of seventeen summers,
Black were her eyes as the berry that grows on the thorn by the
        wayside,
Black, yet how softly they gleamed beneath the brown shade of her
        tresses!
Sweet was her breath as the breath of kine that feed in the meadows.
When in the harvest heat she bore to the reapers at noontide
Flagons of home-brewed ale, ah! fair in sooth was the maiden.
Fairer was she when, on Sunday morn, while the bell from its turret
Sprinkled with holy sounds the air, as the priest with his hyssop
Sprinkles the congregation, and scatters blessings upon them,
Down the long street she passed, with her chaplet of beads and her
        missal,
Wearing her Norman cap, and her kirtle of blue, and the ear-rings,
Brought in the olden time from France, and since, as an heirloom,
Handed down from mother to child, through long generations.
But a celestial brightness—a more ethereal beauty—
Shone on her face and encircled her form, when, after confession,
Homeward serenely she walked with God's benediction upon her.
When she had passed it seemed like the ceasing of exquisite music.
Firmly builded with rafters of oak, the house of the farmer
Stood on the side of a hill commanding the sea; and a shady
Sycamore grew by the door, with a woodbine wreathing around it.
Rudely carved was the porch, with seats beneath; and a footpath
Led through an orchard wide, and disappeared in the meadow.

Under the sycamore tree were hives overhung by a penthouse,
Such as the traveler sees in regions remote by the roadside,
Built o'er a box for the poor, or the blessed image of Mary;
Farther down, on the slope of the hill, was the well with its moss-
    grown
Bucket, fastened with iron, and near it a trough for the horses.
Shielding the house from storms, on the north, were the barns and
    the farmyard,
There stood the broad-wheeled wains and the antique ploughs and the
    harrows;
There were the folds for the sheep; and there, in his feathered
    seraglio,
Strutted the lordly turkey, and crowed the cock, with the selfsame
Voice that in ages of old had startled the penitent Peter.
Bursting with hay were the barns, themselves a village. In each one
Far o'er the gable projected a roof of thatch; and a staircase,
Under the sheltering eaves, led up to the odorous corn-loft.
There too the dove-cot stood, with its meek and innocent inmates
Murmuring ever of love; while above in the variant breezes
Numberless noisy weathercocks rattled and sang of mutation.

Thus, at peace with God and the world, the farmer of Grand-Pré
Lived on his sunny farm, and Evangeline governed his household.
Many a youth, as he knelt in the church and opened his missal,
Fixed his eyes upon her as the saint of his deepest devotion;
Happy was he who might touch her hand or the hem of her garment!
Many a suitor came to her door, by the darkness befriended,
And, as he knocked and waited to hear the sound of her footsteps,
Knew not which beat the louder, his heart or the knocker of iron;
Or at the joyous feast of the Patron Saint of the village,
Bolder grew, and pressed her hand in the dance as he whispered
Hurried words of love, that seemed a part of the music.
But among all who came, young Gabriel only was welcome;
Gabriel Lajeunesse, the son of Basil the blacksmith,
Who was a mighty man in the village, and honored of all men;
For, since the birth of time, throughout all ages and nations,
Has the craft of the smith been held in repute by the people.
Basil was Benedict's friend. Their children from earliest childhood
Grew up together as brother and sister; and Father Felician,

Priest and pedagogue both in the village, had taught them their letters
Out of the self-same book, with the hymns of the church and the
    plain-song.
But when the hymn was sung, and the daily lesson completed,
Swiftly they hurried away to the forge of Basil the blacksmith.
There at the door they stood, with wondering eyes to behold him
Take in his leathern lap the hoof of the horse as a plaything,
Nailing the shoe in its place; while near him the tire of the cart-wheel
Lay like a fiery snake, coiled around in a circle of cinders.
Oft on autumnal eves, when without in the gathering darkness
Bursting with light seemed the smithy, through every cranny and
    crevice,
Warm by the forge within they watched the laboring bellows,
And as its panting ceased, and the sparks expired in the ashes,
Merrily laughed and said they were nuns going into the chapel.
Oft on sledges in winter, as swift as the swoop of the eagle,
Down the hillside bounding, they glided away o'er the meadow.
Oft in the barns they climbed to the populous nests on the rafters,
Seeking with eager eyes that wondrous stone, which the swallow
Brings from the shore of the sea to restore the sight of its fledglings;
Lucky was he who found that stone in the nest of the swallow!
Thus passed a few swift years and they no longer were children.
He was a valiant youth, and his face, like the face of the morning,
Gladdened the earth with its light, and ripened thought into action.
She was a woman now, with the heart and hopes of a woman.
" Sunshine of Saint Eulalie " was she called; for that was the sun-
    shine
Which, as the farmers believed, would load their orchards with
    apples;—
She, too, would bring to her husband's house delight and abundance,
Filling it full of love and the ruddy faces of children.

II.

  Now had the season returned, when the nights grew colder and
    longer,
And the retreating sun the sign of the Scorpion enters.
Birds of passage sailed through the leaden air from the ice-bound,
Desolate northern bays to the shores of tropical islands.

Harvests were gathered in; and wild with the winds of September
Wrestled the trees of the forest, as Jacob of old with the angel.
All the signs foretold a winter long and inclement.
Bees, with prophetic instinct of want, had hoarded their honey
Till the hives overflowed; and the Indian hunters asserted
Cold would the winter be, for thick was the fur of the foxes.
Such was the advent of autumn. Then followed that beautiful season,
Called by the pious Acadian peasants the Summer of All-Saints!
Filled was the air with a dreamy and magical light; and the landscape
Lay as if new created in all the freshness of childhood.
Peace seemed to reign upon earth, and the restless heart of the ocean
Was for a moment consoled. All sounds were in harmony blended.
Voices of children at play, the crowing of cocks in the farm-yards,
Whir of wing in the drowsy air, and the cooing of pigeons,
All were subdued and low as the murmurs of love, and the great sun
Looked with the eye of love through the golden vapors around him;
While arrayed in its robes of russet and scarlet and yellow,
Bright with the sheen of the dew, each glittering tree of the forest
Flashed like the plane-tree the Persian adorned with mantels and
        jewels.

Now recommenced the region of rest and affection and stillness.
Day with its burden and heat had departed, and twilight descending
Brought back the evening star to the sky, and the herds to the home-
        stead.
Pawing the ground they came, and resting their necks on each other,
And with their nostrils distended inhaling the freshness of evening;
Foremost bearing the bell, Evangeline's beautiful heifer,
Proud of her snow-white hide, and the ribbon that waved from her
        collar,
Quietly paced and slow, as if conscious of human affection.
Then came the shepherd back with his bleating flocks from the seaside
Where was their favorite pasture. Behind them followed the watch-
        dog,
Patient, full of importance, and grand in the pride of his instinct,
Walking from side to side with a lordly air, and superbly
Waving his bushy tail, and urging forward the stragglers;
Regent of flocks was he when the shepherd slept; their protector,
When from the forest at night, through the starry silence, the wolves
        howled.

Late, with the rising moon, returned the wains from the marshes,
Laden with briny hay, that filled the air with its odor,
Cheerily neighed the steeds, with dew on their manes and their fet-
        locks,
While aloft on their shoulders the wooden and ponderous saddles,
Painted with brilliant dyes, and adorned with tassels of crimson,
Nodded in bright array, like hollyhocks heavy with blossoms.
Patiently stood the cows meanwhile, and yielded their udders
Unto the mildmaid's hand; whilst loud and in regular cadence
Into the sounding pails the foaming streamlets descended.
Lowing of cattle and peals of laughter were heard in the farm-yard,
Echoed back by the barns. Anon they sank into stillness;
Heavily closed, with a jarring sound, the valves of the barn-doors,
Rattled the wooden bars, and all for a season was silent.

    Indoors, warm by the wide-mouthed fireplace, idly the farmer
Sat in his elbow-chair, and watched how the flames and the smoke-
        wreaths
Struggled together like foes in a burning city. Behind him,
Nodding and mocking along the wall, with gestures fantastic,
Darted his own huge shadow, and vanished away into darkness.
Faces, clumsily carved in oak, on the back of his arm-chair
Laughed in the flickering light, and the pewter plates on the dresser
Caught and reflected the flame, as shields of armies the sunshine.
Fragments of song the old man sang, and carols of Christmas,
Such as at home, in the olden time, his fathers before him
Sang in their Norman orchards and bright Burgundian vineyards.
Close at her father's side was the gentle Evangeline seated,
Spinning flax for the loom, that stood in the corner behind her.
Silent awhile were its treadles, at rest was its diligent shuttle,
While the monotonous drone of the wheel, like the drone of a bagpipe,
Followed the old man's song, and united the fragments together.
As in a church when the chant of the choir at intervals ceases,
Footfalls are heard in the aisles, or words of the priest at the altar,
So, in each pause of the song, with measured motion the clock clicked.

    Thus as they sat, there were footsteps heard, and, suddenly lifted,
Sounded the wooden latch, and the door swung back on its hinges.
Benedict knew by the hob-nailed shoes it was Basil the blacksmith,

And by her beating heart Evangeline knew who was with him.
" Welcome ! " the farmer exclaimed, as their footsteps paused on the
       threshold,
" Welcome, Basil, my friend! Come, take thy place on the settle
Close by the chimney side, which is always empty without thee;
Take from the shelf overhead thy pipe and the box of tobacco;
Never so much thyself art thou as when through the curling
Smoke of the pipe or the forge thy friendly and jovial face gleams
Round and red as the harvest moon through the mist of the marshes."
Then, with a smile of content, thus answered Basil the blacksmith,
Taking with easy air the accustomed seat by the fireside:—
" Benedict Bellefontaine, thou hast ever thy jest and thy ballad!
Ever in cheerfullest mood art thou, when others are filled with
Gloomy forebodings of ill, and see only ruin before them.
Happy art thou, as if every day thou hadst picked up a horseshoe."
Pausing a moment to take the pipe that Evangeline brought him,
And with a coal from the embers had lighted, he slowly continued:—
" Four days now are passed since the English ships at their anchors
Ride in the Gaspereau's mouth, with their cannon pointed against us.
What their design may be is unknown; but all are commanded
On the morrow to meet in the church, where his Majesty's mandate
Will be proclaimed as law in the land. Alas! in the meantime
Many surmises of evil alarm the hearts of the people."
Then made answer the farmer:—" Perhaps some friendlier purpose
Brings these ships to our shores. Perhaps the harvests in England
By untimely rains or untimelier heat have been blighted,
And from our bursting barns they would feed their cattle and chil-
       dren."
" Not so thinketh the folk in the village," said, warmly, the black-
       smith,
Shaking his head, as in doubt; then, heaving a sigh, he continued:—
" Louisburg is not forgotten, nor Beau Séjour, nor Port Royal.
Many already have fled to the forest, and lurk on its outskirts,
Waiting with anxious hearts the dubious fate of to-morrow.
Arms have been taken from us, and warlike weapons of all kinds;
Nothing is left but the blacksmith's sledge and the scythe of the
       mower."
Then with a pleasant smile made answer the jovial farmer:—
" Safer are we unarmed, in the midst of our flocks and our cornfields,

Safer within these peaceful dikes, besieged by the ocean,
Than our fathers in forts, besieged by the enemy's cannon.
Fear no evil, my friend, and to-night may no shadow of sorrow
Fall on this house and hearth; for this is the night of the contract.
Built are the house and the barn. The merry lads of the village
Strongly have built them and well; and, breaking the glebe round
      about them,
Filled the barn with hay, and the house with food for a twelvemonth.
René Leblanc will be here anon, with his papers and inkhorn.
Shall we not then be glad, and rejoice in the joy of our children ? "
As apart by the window she stood, with her hand in her lover's,
Blushing Evangeline heard the words that her father had spoken,
And as they died on his lips, the worthy notary entered.

III.

Bent like a laboring oar, that toils in the surf of the ocean,
Bent, but not broken, by age was the form of the notary public;
Shocks of yellow hair, like the silken floss of the maize, hung
Over his shoulders; his forehead was high; and glasses with horn
      bows
Sat astride on his nose, with a look of wisdom supernal.
Father of twenty children was he, and more than a hundred
Children's children rode on his knee, and heard his great watch tick.
Four long years in the times of the war had he languished a captive,
Suffering much in an old French fort as the friend of the English.
Now, though warier grown, without all guile or suspicion,
Ripe in wisdom was he, but patient, and simple, and childlike,
He was beloved by all, the most of all by the children;
For he told them tales of the Loup-garou in the forest,
And of the goblin that came in the night to water the horses,
And of the white Létiche, the ghost of a child who unchristened
Died, and was doomed to haunt unseen the chambers of children;
And how on Christmas eve the oxen talked in the stable,
And how the fever was cured by a spider shut up in a nutshell,
And of the marvellous powers of four-leaved clover and horseshoes,
With whatsoever else was writ in the lore of the village.
Then up rose from his seat by the fireside Basil the blacksmith,
Knocked from his pipe the ashes, and slowly extending his right hand,

" Father Leblanc," he exclaimed, " thou hast heard the talk in the
        village,
And, perchance, canst tell us some news of these ships and their
        errand."
Then with modest demeanor made answer the notary public,—
" Gossip enough have I heard, in sooth, yet am never the wiser;
And what their errand may be I know no better than others.
Yet am I not of those who imagine some evil intention,
Brings them here, for we are at peace; and why then molest us ? "
" God's name ! " shouted the hasty and somewhat irascible blacksmith;
" Must we in all things look for the how, and the why, and the where-
        fore ?
Daily injustice is done, and might is the right of the strongest ! "
But, without heeding his warmth, continued the notary public,—
" Man is unjust, but God is just, and finally justice
Triumphs; and well I remember a story, that often consoled me.
When as a captive I lay in the old French fort at Port Royal."
This was the old man's favorite tale, and he loved to repeat it
When his neighbors complained that any injustice was done them.
" Once in an ancient city, whose name I no longer remember,
Raised aloft on a column, a brazen statue of Justice
Stood in the public square, upholding the scales in its left hand.
And in its right a sword, as an emblem that justice presided
Over the laws of the land, and the hearts and homes of the people.
Even the birds had built their nests in the scales of the balance,
Having no fear of the sword that flashed in the sunshine above them.
But in the course of time the laws of the land were corrupted;
Might took the place of right, and the weak were oppressed, and the
        mighty
Ruled with an iron rod. Then it chanced in a nobleman's palace
That a necklace of pearls was lost, and ere long a suspicion
Fell on an orphan girl who lived as maid in the household.
She, after form of trial condemned to die on the scaffold,
Patiently met her doom at the foot of the statue of Justice.
As to her Father in heaven her innocent spirit ascended,
Lo! o'er the city a tempest rose; and the bolts of the thunder
Smote the statue of bronze, and hurled in wrath from its left hand
Down on the pavement below the clattering scales of the balance,
And in the hollow thereof was found the nest of a magpie,

Into whose clay-built walls the necklace of pearls was inwoven."
Silenced, but not convinced, when the story was ended, the blacksmith
Stood like a man who fain would speak, but findeth no language;
All his thoughts were congealed into lines on his face, as the vapors
Freeze in fantastic shapes on the window-panes in the winter.

Then Evangeline lighted the brazen lamp on the table,
Filled, till it over-flowed, the pewter tankard with home-brewed
Nut-brown ale, that was famed for its strength in the village of
     Grand-Pré;
While from his pocket the notary drew his papers and inkhorn,
Wrote with a steady hand the date and the age of the parties,
Naming the dower of the bride in flocks of sheep and in cattle.
Orderly all things proceeded, and duly and well were completed,
And the great seal of the law was set like a sun on the margin.
Then from his leathern pouch the farmer threw on the table
Three times the old man's fee in solid pieces of silver;
And the notary rising, and blessing the bride and the bridegroom,
Lifted aloft the tankard of ale and drank to their welfare.
Wiping the foam from his lip he solemnly bowed and departed.
While in silence the others sat and mused by the fireside.
Till Evangeline brought the draught-board out of its corner,
Soon the game begun. In friendly contention the old men
Laughed at each lucky hit, or unsuccessful manœuvre.
Laughed when a man was crowned, or a breach was made in the
     king-row.
Meanwhile apart in the twilight's gloom of a window's embrasure,
Sat the lovers, and whispered together, beholding the moon rise
Over the pallid sea and the silvery mist of the meadows.
Silently one by one, in the infinite meadows of heaven,
Blossomed the lovely stars, the forget-me-nots of the angels.

Thus was the evening passed. Anon the bell from the belfry
Rang out the hour of nine, the village curfew, and straightway
Rose the guests and departed; and silence reigned in the household.
Many a farewell word and sweet good-night on the doorstep
Lingered long in Evangeline's heart, and filled it with gladness.
Carefully then were covered the embers that glowed on the hearth-
     stone,

And on the oaken stairs resounded the tread of the farmer.
Soon with a soundless step the foot of Evangeline followed.
Up the staircase moved a luminous space in the darkness,
Lighted less by the lamp than the shining face of the maiden.
Silent she passed through the hall, and entered the door of her chamber.
Simple that chamber was, with its curtains of white, and its clothes-
        press
Ample and high, on whose spacious shelves were carefully folded
Linen and woollen stuffs, by the hand of Evangeline woven.
This was the precious dower she would bring to her husband in
        marriage,
Better than flocks and herds, being proofs of her skill as a housewife.
Soon she extinguished her lamp, for the mellow and radiant moonlight
Streamed through the windows, and lighted the room, till the heart
        of the maiden
Swelled and obeyed its power, like the tremulous tides of the ocean.
Ah! she was fair, exceeding fair to behold, as she stood with
Naked snow-white feet on the gleaming floor of her chamber!
Little she dreamed that below, among the trees of the orchard,
Waited her lover and watched for the gleam of her lamp and her
        shadow.
Yet were her thoughts of him, and at times a feeling of sadness
Passed o'er her soul, as the sailing shade of clouds in the moonlight
Flitted across the floor and darkened the room for a moment.
And, as she gazed from the window, she saw serenely the moon pass
Forth from the folds of a cloud, and one star followed her footsteps,
As out of Abraham's tent young Ishmael wandered with Hagar!

IV.

Pleasantly rose next morn the sun on the village of Grand-Pré.
Pleasantly gleamed in the soft, sweet air the Basin of Minas,
Where the ships, with their wavering shadows, were riding at anchor.
Life had long been astir in the village, and clamorous labor
Knocked with its hundred hands at the golden gates of the morning.
Now from the country around, from the farms and neighboring ham-
        lets,
Came in their holiday dresses, the blithe Acadian peasants;
Many a glad good-morrow and jocund laugh from the young folk

Made the bright air brighter, as up from the numerous meadows,
Where no path could be seen but the track of wheels in the green-
       sward,
Group after group appeared, and joined, or passed on the highway.
Long ere noon, in the village all sounds of labor were silenced.
Thronged were the streets with people; and noisy groups at the
       house-doors
Sat in the cheerful sun, and rejoiced and gossiped together.
Every house was an inn, where all were welcomed and feasted;
For with this simple people, who lived like brothers together,
All things were held in common, and what one had was another's.
Yet under Benedict's roof hospitality seemed more abundant:
For Evangeline stood among the guests of her father;
Bright was her face with smiles, and words of welcome and gladness
Fell from her beautiful lips, and blessed the cup as she gave it.

Under the open sky, in the odorous air of the orchard,
Stript of its golden fruit, was spread the feast of betrothal.
There in the shade of the porch were the priest and the notary seated:
There good Benedict sat, and sturdy Basil the blacksmith.
Not far withdrawn from these, by the cider-press and the bee-hives,
Michael the fiddler was placed, with the gayest of hearts and of waist-
       coats.
Shadow and light from the leaves alternately played on his snow-white
Hair, as it waved in the wind; and the jolly face of the fiddler
Glowed like a living coal when the ashes are blown from the embers.
Gayly the old man sang to the vibrant sound of his fiddle,
Tous les Bourgeois de Chartres, and Le Carillon de Dunkerque,
And anon with his wooden shoes beat time to the music.
Merrily, merrily whirled the wheels of the dizzying dances
Under the orchard-trees and down the path to the meadows,
Old folk and young together, and children mingled among them.
Fairest of all the maids was Evangeline, Benedict's daughter!
Noblest of all the youths was Gabriel, son of the blacksmith!

So passed the morning away. And lo! with a summon sonorous
Sounded the bell from its tower, and over the meadows a drum beat.
Thronged ere long was the church with men. Without in the church-
       yard,

Waited the women. They stood by the graves, and hung on the head-
        stones
Garlands of autumn-leaves and evergreens fresh from the forest.
Then came the guard from the ships, and marching proudly among
        them
Entered the sacred portal. With loud and dissonant clangor
Echoed the sound of their brazen drums from ceiling and casement,—
Echoed a moment only, and slowly the ponderous portal
Closed, and in silence the crowd awaited the will of the soldiers.
Then uprose their commander, and spake from the steps of the altar,
Holding aloft in his hands, with its seals, the royal commission.
" You are convened this day," he said, " by his Majesty's orders.
Clement and kind has he been; but how you have answered his kind-
        ness,
Let your own hearts reply! To my natural make and my temper
Painful the task is I do, which to you I know must be grievous.
Yet must I bow and obey, and deliver the will of our monarch;
Namely, that all your lands, and dwellings, and cattle of all kinds
Forfeited be to the crown; and that you yourselves from this province
Be transported to other lands. God grant you may dwell there
Ever as faithful subjects, a happy and peaceable people!
Prisoners now I declare you; for such is his Majesty's pleasure ! "
As, when the air is serene in the sultry solstice of summer,
Suddenly gathers a storm, and the deadly sling of the hailstones
Beats down the farmer's corn in the field and shatters his windows,
Hiding the sun, and strewing the ground with thatch from the house-
        roofs,
Bellowing fly the herds, and seek to break their enclosures;
So on the hearts of the people descended the words of the speaker.
Silent a moment they stood in speechless wonder, and then rose
Louder and ever louder a wail of sorrow and anger,
And, by one impulse moved, they madly rushed to the door-way.
Vain was the hope of escape; and cries and fierce imprecations
Rang through the house of prayer; and high o'er the heads of the
        others
Rose, with his arms uplifted, the figure of Basil the blacksmith,
As, on a stormy sea, a spar is tossed by the billows.
Flushed was his face and distorted with passion; and wildly he
        shouted,—

" Down with the tyrants of England; we never have sworn them
        allegiance !
Death to these foreign soldiers, who seize on our homes and our har-
        vests ! "
More he fain would have said, but the merciless hand of a soldier
Smote him upon the mouth, and dragged him down to the pavement.

In the midst of the strife and tumult of angry contention,
Lo! the door of the chancel opened, and Father Felician
Entered, with serious mien, and ascended the steps of the altar,
Raising his reverend hand, with a gesture he awed into silence
All that clamorous throng; and thus he spake to his people;
Deep were his tones and solemn; in accents measured and mournful
Spake he, as, after the tocsin's alarum, distinctly the clock strikes.
" What is this that ye do, my children? what madness has seized you?
Forty years of my life have I labored among you, and taught you,
Not in word alone, but in deed, to love one another!
Is this the fruit of my toils, of my vigils and prayers and privations?
Have you so soon forgotten all lessons of love and forgiveness?
This is the house of the Prince of Peace, and would you profane it
Thus with violent deeds and hearts overflowing with hatred?
Lo! where the crucified Christ from his cross is gazing upon you!
See! in those sorrowful eyes what meekness and holy compassion!
Hark! how those lips still repeat the prayer, ' O Father, forgive
        them ! '
Let us repeat that prayer in the hour when the wicked assail us,
Let us repeat it now, and say, ' O Father, forgive them ! ' "
Few were his words of rebuke, but deep in the hearts of his people
Sank they, and sobs of contrition succeeded the passionate outbreak,
While they repeated his prayer, and said, " O Father, forgive them ! "

Then came the evening service. The tapers gleamed from the altar.
Fervent and deep was the voice of the priest, and the people re-
        sponded,
Not with their lips alone, but their hearts; and the Ave Maria
Sang they, and fell on their knees, and their souls, with devotion
        translated,
Rose on the ardor of prayer, like Elijah ascending to heaven.

   Meanwhile had spread in the village the tidings of ill, and on all
        sides
Wandered, wailing, from house to house the women and children.
Long at her father's door Evangeline stood, with her right-hand
Shielding her eyes from the level rays of the sun, that, descending,
Lighted the village street with mysterious splendor, and roofed each
Peasant's cottage with golden thatch, and emblazoned its windows.
Long within had been spread the snow-white cloth on the table;
There stood the wheaten loaf, and the honey fragrant with wild
        flowers;
There stood the tankard of ale, and the cheese fresh brought from the
        dairy;
And, at the head of the board, the great armchair of the farmer.
Thus did Evangeline wait at her father's door, as the sunset
Threw the long shadows of trees o'er the broad ambrosial meadows.
Ah! on her spirit within a deeper shadow had fallen,
And from the fields of her soul a fragrance celestial ascended,—
Charity, meekness, love and hope, and forgiveness, and patience!
Then, all-forgetful of self, she wandered into the village,
Cheering with looks and words the mournful hearts of the women,
As o'er the darkening fields with lingering steps they departed,
Urged by their household cares, and the weary feet of their children.
Down sank the great red sun, and in golden, glimmering vapors
Veiled the light of his face, like a Prophet descending from Sinai.
Sweetly over the village the bell of the Angelus sounded.

   Meanwhile, amid the gloom, by the church Evangeline lingered.
All was silent within; and in vain at the doors and the windows
Stood she, and listened and looked, till, overcome by emotion,
" Gabriel ! " cried she aloud with tremulous voice; but no answer
Came from the graves of the dead, nor the gloomier grave of the liv-
        ing.
Slowly at length she returned to the tenantless house of her father.
Smouldered the fire on the hearth, on the board was the supper un-
        tasted.
Empty and drear was each room, and haunted with phantoms of
        terror.
Sadly echoed her step on the stair and the floor of her chamber.
In the dead of the night she heard the disconsolate rain fall

Loud on the withered leaves of the sycamore tree by the window.
Keenly the lightning flashed; and the voice of the echoing thunder
Told her that God was in heaven, and governed the world he created!
Then she remembered the tale she had heard of the justice of
        Heaven;
Soothed was her troubled soul, and she peacefully slumbered till
        morning.

V.

Four times the sun had risen and set; and now on the fifth day
Cheerily called the cock to the sleeping maids of the farm-house.
Soon o'er the yellow fields, in silent and mournful procession,
Came from the neighboring hamlets and farms the Acadian women,
Driving in ponderous wains their household goods to the sea-shore,
Pausing and looking back to gaze once more on their dwellings,
Ere they were shut from sight by the winding road and the woodland.
Close at their sides their children ran, and urged on the oxen,
While in their little hands they clasped some fragments of play-
        things.

Thus to the Gaspereau's mouth they hurried and there on the sea-
        beach
Piled in confusion lay the household goods of the peasants.
All day long between the shore and the ships did the boats ply;
All day long the wains came laboring down from the village.
Late in the afternoon when the sun was near to his setting,
Echoed far o'er the fields came the roll of drums from the churchyard.
Thither the women and children thronged. On a sudden the church-
        doors
Opened, and forth came the guard, and marching in gloomy procession
Followed the long-imprisoned, but patient, Acadian farmers.
Even as pilgrims, who journey afar from their homes and their coun-
        try,
Sing as they go, and in singing forget they are weary and wayworn,
So with songs on their lips the Acadian peasants descended
Down from the church to the shore, amid their wives and their
        daughters.
Foremost the young men came; and, raising together their voices,

Sang with tremulous lips a chant of the Catholic Missions:—
"Sacred heart of the Saviour!   O inexhaustible fountain!
Fill our hearts this day with strength and submission and patience ! "
Then the old men, as they marched, and the women that stood by the
          wayside
Joined in the sacred psalm, and the birds in the sunshine above them
Mingled their notes therewith, like voices of spirits departed.

  Half-way down to the shore Evangeline waited in silence,
Not overcome with grief, but strong in the hour of affliction,—
Calmly and sadly she waited, until the procession approached her,
And she beheld the face of Gabriel pale with emotion.
Tears then filled her eyes, and, eagerly running to meet him,
Clasped she his hands, and laid her head on his shoulder, and whis-
          pered,—
" Gabriel! be of good cheer! for if we love one another
Nothing, in truth, can harm us, whatever mischances may happen ! "
Smiling she spake these words; then suddenly paused, for her father
Saw she slowly advancing. Alas! how changed was his aspect!
Gone was the glow from his cheek, and the fire from his eye, and his
          footstep
Heavier seemed with the weight of the heavy heart in his bosom.
But with a smile and a sigh, she clasped his neck and embraced him,
Speaking words of endearment where words of comfort availed not.
Thus to the Gaspereau's mouth moved on that mournful procession.

  There disorder prevailed, and the tumult and stir of embarking.
Busily plied the freighted boats; and in the confusion
Wives were torn from their husbands, and mothers, too late, saw
          their children
Left on the land, extending their arms, with wildest entreaties.
So unto separate ships were Basil and Gabriel carried,
While in despair on the shore Evangeline stood with her father.
Half the task was not done when the sun went down, and the twilight
Deepened and darkened around; and in haste the refluent ocean
Fled away from the shore, and left the line of the sand-beach
Covered with waifs of the tide, with kelp and the slippery sea-weed.
Farther back in the midst of the household goods and the wagons,
Like to a gypsy camp, or a leaguer after a battle,

All escape cut off by the sea, and the sentinels near them,
Lay encamped for the night the houseless Acadian farmers.
Back to its nethermost caves retreated the bellowing ocean,
Dragging adown the beach the rattling pebbles, and leaving
Inland and far up the shore the stranded boats and the sailors.
Then, as the night descended, the herds returned from their pastures;
Sweet was the moist still air with the odor of milk from their udders;
Lowing they waited, and long, at the well-known bars of the farm-
       yard,—
Waited and looked in vain for the voice and the hand of the milkmaid,
Silence reigned in the streets; from the church no Angelus sounded,
Rose no smoke from the roofs, and gleamed no lights from the win-
       dows.

But on the shores meanwhile the evening fires had been kindled.
Built of the drift-wood thrown on the sands from wrecks in the
       tempest.
Round them shades of gloom and sorrowful faces were gathered,
Voices of women were heard, and of men, and the crying of children.
Onward from fire to fire, as from hearth to hearth in his parish,
Wandered the faithful priest, consoling and blessing and cheering,
Like unto shipwrecked Paul on Melita's desolate sea-shore.
Thus he approached the place where Evangeline sat with her father,
And in the flickering light beheld the face of the old man,
Haggard and hollow and wan, and without either thought or emotion,
E'en as the face of a clock from which the hands have been taken.
Vainly Evangeline strove with words and caresses to cheer him,
Vainly offered him food; yet he moved not, he looked not, he spake
       not,
But, with a vacant stare, ever glanced at the flickering firelight.
" Benedicite ! " murmured the priest, in tones of compassion.
More he fain would have said, but his heart was full, and his accents
Faltered and paused on his lips, as the feet of a child on the threshold,
Hushed by the scene he beholds, and the awful presence of sorrow.
Silently, therefore, he laid his hand on the head of the maiden,
Raising his tearful eyes to the silent stars that above them
Moved on their way, unperturbed by the wrongs and sorrows of
       mortals.
Then sat he down by her side, and they wept together in silence.

Suddenly rose from the south a light, as in autumn the blood-red
Moon climbs the crystal walls of heaven, and o'er the horizon
Titan-like stretches its hundred hands upon mountain and meadow,
Seizing the rocks and the rivers, and piling huge shadows together.
Broader and ever broader it gleamed on the roofs of the village,
Gleamed on the sky and the sea, and the ships that lay in the road-
    stead.
Columns of shining smoke uprose, and flashes of flame were
Thrust through their folds and withdrawn, like the quivering hands
    of a martyr.
Then as the wind seized the gleeds and the burning thatch, and, up-
    lifting,
Whirled them aloft through the air, at once from a hundred housetops
Started the sheeted smoke with flashes of flame intermingled.

  These things beheld in dismay the crowd on the shore and on ship-
    board.
Speechless at first they stood, then cried aloud in their anguish,
" We shall behold no more our homes in the village of Grand-Pré ! "
Loud on a sudden the cocks began to crow in the farm-yards,
Thinking the day had dawned; and anon the lowing of cattle
Came on the evening breeze, by the barking of dogs interrupted.
Then rose a sound of dread, such as startles the sleepy encampments
Far in the western prairies or forests that skirt the Nebraska,
When the wild horses affrighted sweep by with the speed of the whirl-
    wind,
Or the loud bellowing herd of buffaloes rush to the river.
Such was the sound that arose on the night, as the herds and the
    horses
Broke through their folds and fences, and madly rushed o'er the
    meadows.

  Overwhelmed with the sight, yet speechless, the priest and the
    maiden
Gazed on the scene of terror that reddened and widened before them;
And as they turned at length to speak to their silent companion,
Lo! from his seat he had fallen, and stretched abroad on the sea-shore
Motionless lay his form, from which the soul had departed.
Slowly the priest uplifted the lifeless head, and the maiden

Knelt at her father's side, and wailed aloud in her terror.
Then in a swoon she sank, and lay with her head on his bosom.
Through the long night she lay in deep, oblivious slumber;
And when she woke from the trance, she beheld a multitude near her.
Faces of friends she beheld, that were mournfully gazing upon her,
Pallid, with tearful eyes, and looks of saddest compassion.
Still the blaze of the burning village illumined the landscape,
Reddened the sky overhead, and gleamed on the faces around her,
And like the day of doom it seemed to her wavering senses.
Then a familiar voice she heard, as it said to the people,—
"Let us bury him here by the sea. When a happier season
Brings us again to our homes from the unknown land of our exile,
Then shall his sacred dust be piously laid in the churchyard."
Such were the words of the priest. And there in haste by the sea-
        side,
Having the glare of the burning village for funeral torches,
But without bell or book, they buried the farmer of Grand-Pré.
And as the voice of the priest repeated the service of sorrow,
Lo! with a mournful sound, like the voice of a vast congregation,
Solemnly answered the sea, and mingled its roar with the dirges.
'Twas the returning tide, that afar from the waste of the ocean,
With the first dawn of the day, came heaving and hurrying landward.
Then recommenced once more the stir and noise of embarking;
And with the ebb of the tide the ships sailed out of the harbor,
Leaving behind them the dead on the shore, and the village in ruins.

PART THE SECOND.

I.

Many a weary year had passed since the burning of Grand-Pré,
When on the falling tide the freighted vessels departed,
Bearing a nation, with all its household gods, into exile,
Exile without an end, and without an example in story.
Far asunder on separate coasts, the Acadians landed,
Scattered were they, like flakes of snow, when the wind from the
      northeast
Strikes aslant through the fogs that darken the Banks of Newfound-
      land.
Friendless, homeless, hopeless, they wandered from city to city,
From the cold lakes of the North to sultry Southern savannas,—
From the bleak shores of the sea to the lands where the Father of
      Waters
Seizes the hills in his hands, and drags them down to the ocean,
Deep in their sands to bury the scattered bones of the mammoth.
Friends they sought and homes, and many, despairing, heart-broken,
Asked of the earth but a grave, and no longer a friend nor a fireside;
Written their history stands on tablets of stone in the churchyards.
Long among them was seen a maiden who waited and wandered,
Lowly and meek in spirit, and patiently suffering all things.
Fair was she and young; but, alas! before her extended,
Dreary and vast and silent, the desert of life, with its pathway
Marked by the graves of those who had sorrowed and suffered before
      her,
Passions long extinguished, and hopes long dead and abandoned,
As the emigrant's way o'er the Western desert is marked by
Camp-fires long consumed, and bones that bleach in the sunshine.
Something there was in her life incomplete, imperfect, unfinished;
As if a morning of June, with all its music and sunshine.
Suddenly paused in the sky, and, fading, slowly descended
Into the east again, from whence it late had arisen.
Sometimes she lingered in towns, till, urged by the fever within her,
Urged by a restless longing, the hunger and thirst of the spirit,
She would commence again her endless search and endeavor;

Sometimes in churchyards strayed, and gazed on the crosses and
tombstones,
Sat by some nameless grave, and thought that perhaps in its bosom
He was already at rest, and she longed to slumber beside him.
Sometimes a rumor, a hearsay, an inarticulate whisper,
Came with its airy hand to point and beckon her forward.
Sometimes she spake with those who had seen her beloved and known
him,
But it was long ago, in some far-off place or forgotten.
"Gabriel Lajeunesse!" they said; "O yes! we have seen him.
He was with Basil the blacksmith, and both have gone to the prairies;
Coureurs-des-Bois are they, and famous hunters and trappers."
"Gabriel Lajeunesse!" said others; "O yes! we have seen him.
He is a Voyageur in the lowlands of Louisiana."
Then would they say, "Dear child! why dream and wait for him
longer?
Are there not other youths as fair as Gabriel? Others
Who have hearts as tender and true, and spirits as loyal?
Here is Baptiste Leblanc, the notary's son, who has loved thee
Many a tedious year; come, give him thy hand and be happy!
Thou art too fair to be left to braid St. Catherine's tresses."
Then would Evangeline answer, serenely but sadly, "I cannot,
Whither my heart has gone, there follows my hand, and not else-
where.
For when the heart goes before, like a lamp, and illumines the path-
way,
Many things are made clear, that else lie hidden in darkness."
Thereupon the priest, her friend and father-confessor,
Said, with a smile, "O daughter! thy God thus speaketh within thee!
Talk not of wasted affection, affection never was wasted;
If it enrich not the heart of another, its waters, returning
Back to their springs, like the rain, shall fill them full of refreshment;
That which the fountain sends forth returns again to the fountain.
Patience; accomplish thy labor; accomplish thy work of affection!
Sorrow and silence are strong, and patient endurance is godlike.
Therefore accomplish thy labor of love, till the heart is made godlike,
Purified, strengthened, perfected, and rendered more worthy of
heaven!"
Cheered by the good man's words, Evangeline labored and waited.

Still in her heart she heard the funeral dirge of the ocean,
But with its sound there was mingled a voice that whispered, " Despair not ! "
Thus did that poor soul wander in want and cheerless discomfort,
Bleeding, barefooted, over the shards and thorns of existence.
Let me essay, O Muse! to follow the wanderer's footsteps;—
Not through each devious path, each changeful year of existence;
But as a traveler follows a streamlet's course through the valley:
Far from its margin at times, and seeing the gleam of its water
Here and there, in some open space, and at intervals only;
Then drawing nearer its banks, through sylvan glooms that conceal it,
Though he behold it not, he can hear its continuous murmur;
Happy, at length, if he find the spot where it reaches an outlet.

II.

It was the month of May. Far down the Beautiful River,
Past the Ohio shore and past the mouth of the Wabash,
Into the golden stream of the broad and swift Mississippi,
Floated a cumbrous boat, that was rowed by Acadian boatmen.
It was a band of exiles; a raft, as it were, from the shipwrecked
Nation, scattered along the coast, now floating together,
Bound by the bonds of a common belief and a common misfortune;
Men and women and children, who, guided by hope or by hearsay,
Sought for their kith and their kin among the few-acred farmers
On the Acadian coast, and the prairies of fair Opelousas.
With them Evangeline went, and her guide, the Father Felician.
Onward o'er sunken sands, through a wilderness sombre with forests,
Day after day they glided adown the turbulent river;
Night after night, by their blazing fires, encamped on its borders.
Now through rushing chutes, among green islands, where plume-like
Cotton-trees nodded their shadowy crests, they swept with the current,
Then emerged into broad lagoons, where silvery sand-bars
Lay in the stream, and along the wimpling waves of their margin,
Shining with snow-like plumes, large flocks of pelicans waded.
Level the landscape grew, and along the shores of the river,
Shaded by china-trees, in the midst of luxuriant gardens,
Stood the houses of planters, with negro-cabins and dove-cots.

They were approaching the region where reigns perpetual summer,
Where through the Golden Coast, and groves of orange and citron,
Sweeps with majestic curve the river away to the eastward.
They, too, swerved from their course; and, entering the Bayou of
       Plaquemine,
Soon were lost in a maze of sluggish and devious waters,
Which, like a network of steel, extended in every direction.
Over their heads the towering and tenebrous boughs of the cypress
Met in a dusky arch, and trailing mosses in mid-air
Waved like banners that hang on the walls of ancient cathedrals.
Deathlike the silence seemed, and unbroken, save by the herons
Home to their roosts in the cedar-trees returning at sunset,
Or by the owl, as he greeted the moon with demoniac laughter.
Lovely the moonlight was as it glanced and gleamed on the water,
Gleamed on the columns of cypress and cedar sustaining the arches,
Down through whose broken vaults it fell as through chinks in a ruin.
Dreamlike, and indistinct, and strange were all things around them;
And o'er their spirits there came a feeling of wonder and sadness,—
Strange forebodings of ill, unseen that cannot be compassed.
As, at the tramp of a horse's hoof on the turf of the prairies,
Far in advance are closed the leaves of the shrinking mimosa,
So, at the hoof-beats of fate, with sad forebodings of evil,
Shrinks and closes the heart, ere the stroke of doom has attained it.
But Evangeline's heart was sustained by a vision, that faintly
Floated before her eyes, and beckoned her on through the moonlight.
It was the thought of her brain that assumed the shape of a phantom.
Through those shadowy isles had Gabriel wandered before her,
And every stroke of the oar now brought him nearer and nearer.

Then in his place, at the prow of the boat, rose one of the oarsmen,
And, as a signal sound, if others like them peradventure,
Sailed on those gloomy and midnight streams, blew a blast on his
       bugle.
Wild through the dark colonnades and corridors leafy the blast rang,
Breaking the seal of silence, and giving tongues to the forest.
Soundless above them the banners of moss just stirred to the music.
Multitudinous echoes awoke and died in the distance,
Over the watery floor, and beneath the reverberant branches;
But not a voice replied; no answer came from the darkness;

And, when the echoes had ceased, like a sense of pain was the silence.
Then Evangeline slept; but the boatmen rowed through the midnight,
Silent at times, then singing familiar Canadian boat-songs,
Such as they sang of old on their own Acadian rivers,
While through the night were heard the mysterious sounds of the
  desert,
Far off,—indistinct,—as of wave or wind in the forest,
Mixed with the whoop of the crane and the roar of the grim alligator.

  Thus ere another noon they emerged from the shades; and before
    them
Lay, in the golden sun, the lakes of the Atchafalaya.
Water-lilies in myriads rocked on the slight undulations
Made by the passing oars, and resplendent in beauty, the lotus
Lifted her golden crown above the heads of the boatmen.
Faint was the air with the odorous breath of magnolia blossoms,
And with the heat of noon; and numberless sylvan islands,
Fragrant and thickly embowered with blossoming edges of roses,
Near to whose shores they glided along, invited to slumber.
Soon by the fairest of these their weary oars were suspended.
Under the boughs of Wachita willows, that grew by the margin,
Safely their boat was moored; and scattered about on the greensward,
Tired with their midnight toil, the weary travelers slumbered.
Over them vast and high extended the cope of a cedar.
Swinging from its great arms, the trumpet-flower and the grapevine
Hung their ladder of ropes aloft like the ladder of Jacob,
On whose pendulous stairs the angels ascending, descending,
Were the swift humming-birds that flitted from blossom to blossom.
Such was the vision Evangeline saw as she slumbered beneath it.
Filled was her heart with love, and the dawn of an opening heaven
Lighted her soul in sleep with the glory of regions celestial.

  Nearer, ever nearer, among the numberless islands,
Darted a light, swift boat, that sped away o'er the water,
Urged on its course by the sinewy arms of hunters and trappers.
Northward its prow was turned, to the land of the bison and beaver,
At the helm sat a youth, with countenance thoughtful and careworn.
Dark and neglected locks overshadowed his brow, and a sadness
Somewhat beyond his years on his face was legibly written.

Gabriel was it, who, weary with waiting, unhappy and restless,
Sought in the western wilds oblivion of self and of sorrow.
Swiftly they glided along, close under the lee of the island,
But by the opposite bank, and behind a screen of palmettos,
So that they saw not the boat, where it lay concealed in the willows,
All undisturbed by the dash of their oars, and unseen, were the
       sleepers.
Angel of God was there none to awaken the slumbering maiden.
Swiftly they glided away, like the shade of a cloud on the prairie.
After the sound of their oars on the tholes had died in the distance,
As from a magic trance the sleepers awoke, and the maiden
Said with a sigh to the friendly priest, "O Father Felician!
Something says in my heart that near me Gabriel wanders.
Is it a foolish dream, an idle and vague superstition,
Or has an angel passed, and revealed the truth to my spirit?"
Then, with a blush, she added, "Alas for my credulous fancy!
Unto ears like thine such words as these have no meaning."
But made answer the reverend man, and he smiled as he answered,—
"Daughter, thy words are not idle; nor are they to me without mean-
       ing.
Feeling is deep and still; and the word that floats on the surface
Is as the tossing buoy, that betrays where the anchor is hidden.
Therefore trust to thy heart, and to what the world calls illusions.
Gabriel truly is near thee; for not far away to the southward,
On the banks of the Téche, are the towns of St. Maur and St. Martin.
There the long-wandering bride shall be given again to her bride-
       groom,
There the long-absent pastor regain his flock and his sheepfold.
Beautiful is the land, with its prairies and forests of fruit-trees;
Under the feet a garden of flowers, and the bluest of heavens
Bending above, and resting its dome on the walls of the forest,
They who dwell there have named it the Eden of Louisiana."

With these words of cheer they arose and continued their journey.
Softly the evening came. The sun from the western horizon
Like a magician extended his golden wand o'er the landscape;
Twinkling vapors arose; and sky and water and forest
Seemed all on fire at the touch, and melted and mingled together.
Hanging between two skies, a cloud with edges of silver,

Floated the boat, with its dripping oars, on the motionless water.
Filled was Evangeline's heart with inexpressible sweetness.
Touched by the magic spell, the sacred fountains of feeling
Glowed with the light of love, as the skies and waters around her.
Then from a neighboring thicket the mocking-bird, wildest of singers,
Swinging aloft on a willow spray that hung o'er the water,
Shook from his little throat such floods of delirious music,
That the whole air and the woods and the waves seemed silent to
    listen.
Plaintive at first were the tones and sad; then soaring to madness
Seemed they to follow or guide the revel of frenzied Bacchantes.
Single notes were then heard, in sorrowful, low lamentation;
Till, having gathered them all, he flung them abroad in derision,
As when, after a storm, a gust of wind through the tree-tops
Shakes down the rattling rain in a crystal shower on the branches.
With such a prelude as this, and hearts that throbbed with emotion,
Slowly they entered the Téche, where it flows through the green
    Opelousas,
And, through the amber air, above the crest of the woodland,
Saw the column of smoke that arose from a neighboring dwelling;—
Sounds of a horn they heard, and the distant lowing of cattle.

III.

Near to the bank of the river, o'ershadowed by oaks, from whose
    branches
Garlands of Spanish moss and of mystic mistletoe flaunted,
Such as the Druids cut down with golden hatchets at Yule-tide,
Stood, secluded and still, the house of the herdsman. A garden
Girded it round about with a belt of luxuriant blossoms,
Filling the air with fragrance. The house itself was of timbers
Hewn from the cypress-tree, and carefully fitted together.
Large and low was the roof, and on slender columns supported,
Rose-wreathed, vine-encircled, a broad and spacious veranda,
Haunt of the humming-bird and the bee, extended around it.
At each end of the house, amid the flowers of the garden,
Stationed the dove-cots were, as love's perpetual symbol,
Scenes of endless wooing, and endless contentions of rivals.
Silence reigned o'er the place. The line of shadow and sunshine

Ran near the tops of the trees, but the house itself was in shadow,
And from its chimney-top, ascending and slowly expanding
Into the evening air, a thin blue column of smoke rose.
In the rear of the house, from the garden gate, ran a pathway
Through the great groves of oak to the skirts of the limitless prairie,
Into whose sea of flowers the sun was slowly descending.
Full in his track of light, like ships with shadowy canvas
Hanging loose from their spars in a motionless calm in the tropics,
Stood a cluster of trees, with tangled cordage of grapevines.

Just where the woodlands met the flowery surf of the prairie,
Mounted upon his horse, with Spanish saddle and stirrups,
Sat a herdsman, arrayed in gaiters and doublet of deerskin.
Broad and brown was the face that from under the Spanish sombrero
Gazed on the peaceful scene, with the lordly look of its master.
Round about him were numberless herds of kine, that were grazing
Quietly in the meadows, and breathing the vapory freshness
That uprose from the river, and spread itself over the landscape.
Slowly lifting the horn that hung at his side, and expanding
Fully his broad, deep chest, he blew a blast, that resounded
Wildly and sweet and far, through the still damp air of the evening.
Suddenly out of the grass the long white horns of the cattle
Rose like flakes of foam on the adverse currents of ocean.
Silent a moment they gazed, then bellowing rushed o'er the prairie
And the whole mass became a cloud, a shade in the distance.
Then, as the herdsman turned to the house, through the gate of the
       garden
Saw he the forms of the priest and the maiden advancing to meet him.
Suddenly down from his horse he sprang in amazement and forward
Rushed with extended arms and exclamations of wonder;
When they beheld his face, they recognized Basil the blacksmith.
Hearty his welcome was, as he led his guests to the garden.
There in an arbor of roses with endless question and answer
Gave they vent to their hearts, and renewed their friendly embraces,
Laughing and weeping by turns, or sitting silent and thoughtful.
Thoughtful, for Gabriel came not; and now dark doubts and mis-
       givings
Stole o'er the maiden's heart; and Basil, somewhat embarrassed,
Broke the silence, and said, "If you came by the Atchafalaya,

How have you nowhere encountered my Gabriel's boat on the
      bayous ? "
Over Evangeline's face at the words of Basil a shade passed.
Tears came into her eyes, and she said, with a tremulous accent,
" Gone ? is Gabriel gone ? " and, concealing her face on his shoulder,
All her overburdened heart gave way, and she wept and lamented.
Then the good Basil said—and his voice grew blithe as he said it,—
" Be of good cheer, my child; it is only to-day he departed.
Foolish boy! he has left me alone with my herds and my horses.
Moody and restless grown, and tried and troubled, his spirit
Could no longer endure the calm of this quiet existence.
Thinking ever of thee, uncertain and sorrowful ever,
Ever silent, or speaking only of thee and his troubles,
He at length had become so tedious to men and to maidens,
Tedious even to me, that at length I bethought me, and sent him
Unto the town of Adayes to trade for mules with the Spaniards.
Thence he will follow the Indian trails to the Ozark Mountains,
Hunting for furs in the forests, on rivers trapping the beaver.
Therefore be of good cheer; we will follow the fugitive lover;
He is not far on his way, and the Fates and the streams are against
      him.
Up and away to-morrow, and through the red dew of the morning
We will follow him fast, and bring him back to his prison."

    Then glad voices were heard, and up from the banks of the river,
Borne aloft on his comrades' arms, came Michael the fiddler.
Long under Basil's roof had he lived like a god on Olympus,
Having no other care than dispensing music to mortals.
Far renowned was he for his silver locks and his fiddle.
" Long live Michael," they cried, " our brave Acadian minstrel ! "
As they bore him aloft in triumphal procession; and straightway
Father Felician advanced with Evangeline, greeting the old man
Kindly and oft, and recalling the past, while Basil, enraptured,
Hailed with hilarious joy his old companions and gossips,
Laughing loud and long, and embracing mothers and daughters.
Much they marveled to see the wealth of the ci-devant blacksmith,
All his domains and his herds, and his patriarchal demeanor;
Much they marveled to hear his tales of the soil and the climate,
And of the prairies, whose numberless herds were his who would take
      them;

Each one thought in his heart, that he, too, would go and do likewise.
Thus they ascended the steps, and, crossing the breezy veranda,
Entered the hall of the house, where already the supper of Basil
Waited his late return; and they rested and feasted together.

Over the joyous feast the sudden darkness descended.
All was silent without, and, illuming the landscape with silver,
Fair rose the dewy moon and the myriad stars; but within doors,
Brighter than these, shone the faces of friends in the glimmering
      lamplight.
Then from his station aloft, at the head of the table, the herdsman
Poured forth his heart and his wine together in endless profusion.
Lighting his pipe, that was filled with sweet Natchitoches tobacco,
Thus he spake to his guests, who listened, and smiled as they lis-
      tened:—
" Welcome once more, my friends, who long have been friendless and
      homeless,
Welcome once more to a home, that is better perchance than the old
      one,
Here no hungry winter congeals our blood like the rivers,
Here no stony ground provokes the wrath of the farmer.
Smoothly the ploughshare runs through the soil, as a keel through
      the water.
All the year round the orange-groves are in blossom; and grass grows
More in a single night than a whole Canadian summer.
Here, too, numberless herds run wild and unclaimed in the prairies;
Here, too, lands may be had for the asking, and forests of timber
With a few blows of the axe are hewn and framed into houses.
After your houses are built, and your fields are yellow with harvests,
No King George of England shall drive you away from your home-
      steads,
Burning your dwellings and barns, and stealing your farms and your
      cattle."
Speaking these words, he blew a wrathful cloud from his nostrils
While his huge brown hand came thundering down on the table,
So that the guests all started; and Father Felician astounded,
Suddenly paused, with a pinch of snuff half-way to his nostrils.
But the brave Basil resumed, and his words were milder and gayer:—
" Only beware of the fever, my friends, beware of the fever!

For it is not like that of our cold Acadian climate,
Cured by wearing a spider hung round one's neck in a nutshell ! "
Then there were voices heard at the door, and footsteps approaching
Sounded upon the stairs and the floor of the breezy veranda.
It was the neighboring Creoles and small Acadian planters,
Who had been summoned all to the house of Basil the herdsman.
Merry the meeting was of ancient comrades and neighbors:
Friend clasped friend in his arms; and they who before were as
          strangers,
Meeting in exile, became straightway as friends to each other,
Drawn by the gentle bond of a common country together.
But in the neighboring hall a strain of music, proceeding
From the accordant strings of Michael's melodious fiddle,
Broke up all further speech. Away, like children delighted,
All things forgotten besides, they gave themselves to the maddening
Whirl of the dizzy dance, as it swept and swayed to the music,
Dreamlike, with beaming eyes and the rush of fluttering garments.

   Meanwhile, apart, at the head of the hall, the priest and the herds-
          man
Sat, conversing together of past and present and future;
While Evangeline stood like one entranced, for within her
Olden memories rose, and loud in the midst of the music
Heard she the sound of the sea, and an irrepressible sadness
Came o'er her heart, and unseen she stole forth into the garden.
Beautiful was the night. Behind the black wall of the forest,
Tipping its summit with silver, arose the moon. On the river
Fell here and there through the branches a tremulous gleam of the
          moonlight,
Like the sweet thoughts of love on a darkened and devious spirit,
Nearer and round about her, the manifold flowers of the garden
Poured out their souls in odors, that were their prayers and confes-
          sions
Unto the night, as it went its way, like a silent Carthusian.
Fuller of fragrance than they, and as heavy with shadows and night-
          dews,
Hung the heart of the maiden. The calm and the magical moonlight
Seemed to inundate her soul with indefinable longings,
As, through the garden gate, and beneath the shade of the oak-trees,

Passed she along the path to the edge of the measureless prairie.
Silent it lay, with a silvery haze upon it, and fire-flies
Gleaming and floating away in mingled and infinite numbers.
Over her head the stars, the thoughts of God in the heavens,
Shone on the eyes of man, who had ceased to marvel and worship,
Save when a blazing comet was seen on the walls of that temple,
As if a hand had appeared and written upon them, "Upharsin."
And the soul of the maiden, between the stars and the fire-flies,
Wandered alone, and she cried, "O Gabriel! O my beloved!
Art thou so near unto me, and yet I cannot behold thee?
Art thou so near unto me, and yet thy voice does not reach me?
Ah! how often thy feet have trod this path to the prairie!
Ah! how often thine eyes have looked on the woodlands around me!
Ah! how often beneath this oak, returning from labor,
Thou hast lain down to rest, and to dream of me in thy slumbers!
When shall these eyes behold, these arms be folded about thee?"
Loud and sudden and near the note of a whippoorwill sounded
Like a flute in the woods; and anon, through the neighboring thickets,
Farther and farther away it floated and dropped into silence.
"Patience!" whispered the oaks from oracular caverns of darkness:
And from the moonlit meadow, a sigh responded "To-morrow!"

Bright rose the sun next day; and all the flowers of the garden
Bathed his shining feet with their tears, and anointed his tresses
With the delicious balm that they bore in their vases of crystal.
"Farewell!" said the priest, as he stood at the shadowy threshold;
"See that you bring us the Prodigal Son from his fasting and famine,
And, too, the Foolish Virgin, who slept when the bridegroom was
    coming."
"Farewell!" answered the maiden, and, smiling, with Basil de-
    scended
Down to the river's brink, where the boatmen already were waiting.
Thus beginning their journey with morning and sunshine, and glad-
    ness,
Swiftly they followed the flight of him who was speeding before
    them,
Blown by the blast of fate like a dead leaf over the desert.
Not that day, nor the next, nor yet the day that succeeded,
Found they trace of his course, in lake or forest or river,

Nor, after many days, had they found him; but vague and uncertain
Rumors alone were their guides through a wild and desolate country;
Till, at the little inn of the Spanish town of Adayes,
Weary and worn, they alighted, and learned from the garrulous land-
      lord,
That on the day before, with horses and guides and companions,
Gabriel left the village and took the road of the prairies.

IV.

Far in the West there lies a desert land, where the mountains
Lift, through perpetual snows, their lofty and luminous summits.
Down from their jagged, deep ravines, where the gorge, like a gate-
      way,
Opens a passing rude to the wheels of the emigrant's wagon,
Westward the Oregon flows and the Walleway and Owyhee.
Eastward, with devious course, among the Wind-river Mountains,
Through the Sweet-water Valley precipitate leaps the Nebraska;
And to the south, from Fontaine-qui-bout and the Spanish sierras,
Fretted with sands and rocks, and swept by the wind of the desert.
Numberless torrents, with ceaseless sound, descend to the ocean,
Like the great chords of a harp, in loud and solemn vibrations.
Spreading between these streams are the wondrous, beautiful prairies,
Billowy bays of grass ever rolling in shadow and sunshine.
Bright with luxuriant clusters of roses and purple amorphas.
Over them wandered the buffalo herds, and the elk and the roebuck,
Over them wandered the wolves, and herds of riderless horses,
Fires that blast and blight, and winds that are weary with travel;
Over them wander the scattered tribes of Ishmael's children,
Staining the desert with blood; and above their terrible war-trails
Circles and sails aloft, on pinions majestic, the vulture,
Like the implacable soul of a chieftain slaughtered in battle,
By invisible stairs ascending and scaling the heavens.
Here and there rise smokes from the camps of these savage marau-
      ders;
Here and there rise groves from the margins of swift-running rivers;
And the grim, taciturn bear, the anchorite monk of the desert,
Climbs down their dark ravines to dig for roots by the brook-side,
And over all is the sky, the clear and crystalline heaven,
Like the protecting hand of God inverted above them.

Into this wonderful land, at the base of the Ozark Mountains,
Gabriel far had entered, with hunters and trappers behind him.
Day after day, with their Indian guides, the maiden and Basil
Followed his flying steps, and thought each day to o'ertake him.
Sometimes they saw, or thought they saw, the smoke of his camp-fire
Rise in the morning air from the distant plain; but at nightfall,
When they had reached the place, they found only embers and ashes.
And, though their hearts were sad at times and their bodies were
      weary,
Hope still guided them on, as the magic Fata Morgana
Showed them her lakes of light, that retreated and vanished before
      them.

Once, as they sat by their evening fire, there silently entered
Into the little camp an Indian woman, whose features
Wore deep traces of sorrow, and patience as great as her sorrow.
She was a Shawnee woman returning home to her people,
From the far off hunting-grounds of the cruel Comanches,
Where her Canadian husband, a Coureur-des-Bois, had been mur-
      dered.
Touched were their hearts at her story, and warmest and friendliest
      welcome
Gave they, with words of cheer, and she sat and feasted among them
On the buffalo meat and the venison cooked on the embers.
But when their meal was done, and Basil and all his companions,
Worn with the long day's march and the chase of the deer and the
      bison,
Stretched themselves on the ground, and slept where the quivering
      firelight
Flashed on their swarthy cheeks, and their forms wrapped up in their
      blankets.
Then at the door of Evangeline's tent she sat and repeated
Slowly, with soft, low voice, and the charm of her Indian accent,
All the tale of her love, with its pleasures, and pains, and reverses.
Much Evangeline wept at the tale, and to know that another
Hapless heart like her own had loved and had been disappointed.
Moved to the depths of her soul by pity and woman's compassion.
Yet in her sorrow pleased that one who had suffered was near her,
She in turn related her love and all its disasters.

Mute with wonder the Shawnee sat, and when she had ended
Still was mute; but at length, as if a mysterious horror
Passed through her brain, she spake, and repeated the tale of the
       Mowis;
Mowis, the bridegroom of snow, who won and wedded a maiden
But, when the morning came, arose and passed from the wigwam,
Fading and melting away and dissolving into the sunshine,
Till she beheld him no more, though she followed far into the forest.
Then, in those sweet, low tones, that seemed like a weird incantation,
Told she the tale of the fair Lilinau, who was wooed by a phantom,
That, through the pines, o'er her father's lodge in the hush of the twi-
       light,
Breathed like the evening wind, and whispered love to the maiden,
Till she followed his green and waving plume through the forest,
And nevermore returned, nor was seen again by her people.
Silent with wonder and strange surprise, Evangeline listened
To the soft flow of her magical words, till the region around her
Seemed like enchanted ground, and her swarthy guest the enchantress.
Slowly over the tops of the Ozark Mountains the moon rose,
Lighting the little tent, and with a mysterious splendor
Touching the sombre leaves, and embracing and filling the woodland.
With a delicious sound the brook rushed by, and the branches
Swayed and sighed overhead in scarcely audible whispers.
Filled with the thoughts of love was Evangeline's heart, but a secret,
Subtile sense crept in of pain and indefinite terror,
As the cold, poisonous snake, creeps into the nest of the swallow.
It was no earthly fear. A breath from the region of spirits
Seemed to float in the air of night; and she felt for a moment
That, like the Indian maid, she, too, was pursuing a phantom.
With this thought she slept, and the fear and the phantom had van-
       ished.

Early upon the morrow the march was resumed; and the Shawnee
Said, as they journeyed along, "On the western slope of these moun-
       tains
Dwells in his little village the Black Robe chief of the Mission.
Much he teaches the people, and tells them of Mary and Jesus;
Loud laugh their hearts with joy, and weep with pain, as they hear
       him."

Then, with a sudden and secret emotion, Evangeline answered,
"Let us go to the Mission, for there good tidings await us ! "
Thither they turned their steeds; and behind a spur of the moun-
        tains,
Just as the sun went down, they heard a murmur of voices,
And in a meadow green and broad, by the bank of a river,
Saw the tents of the Christians, the tents of the Jesuit Mission.
Under a towering oak, that stood in the midst of the village,
Knelt the Black Robe chief with his children. A crucifix fastened
High on the trunk of the tree, and overshadowed by grapevines,
Looked with its agonized face on the multitude kneeling beneath it.
This was their rural chapel. Aloft, through the intricate arches
Of its aerial roof, rose the chant of their vespers,
Mingling its notes with the soft susurrus and sighs of the branches.
Silent, with heads uncovered, the travelers, nearer approaching,
Knelt on the swarded floor, and joined in the evening devotions,
But when the service was done, and the benediction had fallen
Forth from the hands of the priest, like seed from the hands of the
        sower,
Slowly the reverend man advanced to the strangers, and bade them
Welcome; and when they replied, he smiled with benignant expression,
Hearing the homelike sounds of his mother-tongue in the forest
And, with words of kindness, conducted them into his wigwam.
There upon mats and skins they reposed, and on cakes of the maize-
        ear
Feasted, and slaked their thirst from the water-gourd of the teacher.
Soon was their story told; and the priest with solemnity answered:—
"Not six suns have risen and set since Gabriel, seated
On this mat by my side, where now the maiden reposes,
Told me this same sad tale; then arose and continued his journey ! "
Soft was the voice of the priest, and he spake with an accent of
        kindness;
But on Evangeline's heart fell his words as in winter the snow-flakes
Fall into some lone nest from which the birds have departed.
"Far to the north he has gone," continued the priest; "but in au-
        tumn,
When the chase is done, will return again to the Mission."
Then Evangeline said, and her voice was meek and submissive,
"Let me remain with thee, for my soul is sad and afflicted."

So seemed it wise and well unto all; and betimes on the morrow,
Mounting his Mexican steed, with his Indian guides and companions,
Homeward Basil returned, and Evangeline stayed at the Mission.

Slowly, slowly, slowly the days succeeded each other,—
Days and weeks and months! and the fields of maize that were
      springing
Green from the ground when a stranger she came, now waving above
      her,
Lifted their slender shafts, with leaves interlacing, and forming
Cloisters for mendicant crows and granaries pillaged by squirrels.
Then in the golden weather the maize was husked, and the maidens
Blushed at each blood-red ear, for that betokened a lover,
But at the crooked laughed, and called it a thief in the corn-field.
Even the blood-red ear to Evangeline brought not her lover,
" Patience ! " the priest would say; " have faith, and thy prayer will
      be answered!
Look at this vigorous plant that lifts its head from the meadow,
See how its leaves are turned to the north, as true as the magnet;
This is the compass-flower, that the finger of God has planted
Here in the houseless wild, to direct the traveler's journey
Over the sea-like, pathless, limitless waste of the desert.
Such in the soul of man is faith. The blossoms of passion,
Gay and luxuriant flowers, are brighter and fuller of fragrance,
But they beguile us, and lead us astray, and their color is deadly.
Only this humble plant can guide us here, and hereafter
Crown us with asphodel flowers, that are wet with the dews of
      nepenthe."

So came the autumn, and passed, and the winter,—yet Gabriel
      came not;
Blossomed the opening spring, and the notes of the robin and blue-
      bird
Sounded sweet upon wold and in wood, yet Gabriel came not.
But on the breath of the summer winds a rumor was wafted
Sweeter than song of bird, or hue or odor of blossom.
Far to the north and east, it is said, in the Michigan forests,
Gabriel had his lodge by the banks of the Saginaw River.
And, with returning guides, that sought the lakes of St. Lawrence,

Saying a sad farewell, Evangeline went from the Mission.
When over weary ways, by long and perilous marches,
She had attained at length the depths of the Michigan forests,
Found she the hunter's lodge deserted and fallen to ruin!

Thus did the long sad years glide on, and in seasons and places
Divers and distant far was seen the wandering maiden;—
Now in the Tents of Grace of the meek Moravian missions,
Now in the noisy camps and the battle fields of the army,
Now in secluded hamlets, in towns and populous cities.
Like a phantom she came, and passed away unremembered.
Fair was she and young, when in hope began the long journey;
Faded was she and old, when in disappointment it ended.
Each succeeding year stole something away from her beauty,
Leaving behind it, broader and deeper, the gloom and the shadow.
Then there appeared and spread faint streaks of gray o'er her fore-
        head;
Dawn of another life, that broke o'er her earthly horizon,
As in the Eastern sky the first faint streaks of the morning.

V.

In that delightful land which is washed by the Delaware's waters,
Guarding in sylvan shades the name of Penn the apostle,
Stands on the banks of its beautiful stream the city he founded.
There all the air is balm, and the peach is the emblem of beauty,
And the streets still re-echo the names of the trees of the forest,
As if they fain would appease the Dryads whose haunts they molested.
There from the troubled sea had Evangeline landed, an exile,
Finding among the children of Penn a home and a country.
There old René Leblanc had died; and when he departed,
Saw at his side only one of all his hundred descendants.
Something at least there was in the friendly streets of the city,
Something that spake to her heart, and made her no longer a stranger;
And her ear was pleased with the Thee and Thou of the Quakers.
For it recalled the past, the old Acadian country,
Where all men were equal, and all were brothers and sisters.
So, when the fruitless search, the disappointed endeavor,
Ended, to recommence no more upon earth, uncomplaining,

Thither, as leaves to the light, were turned her thoughts and her
    footsteps.
As from a mountain's top the rainy mists of the morning
Roll away and afar we behold the landscape below us,
Sun-illumined, with shining rivers and hamlets,
So fell the mists from her mind, and she saw the world far below her.
Dark no longer, but all illumined with love; and the pathway
Which she had climbed so far, lying smooth and fair in the distance.
Gabriel was not forgotten. Within her heart was his image
Clothed in the beauty of love and youth, as last she beheld him,
Only more beautiful made by his deathlike silence and absence.
Into her thoughts of him time entered not, for it was not.
Over him years had no power; he was not changed, but transfigured;
He had become to her heart as one who is dead, and not absent;
Patience and abnegation of self, and devotion to others,
This was the lesson a life of trial and sorrow had taught her.
So was her love diffused, but, like some odorous spices,
Suffered no waste nor loss, though filling the air with aroma.
Other hope had she none, nor wish in life, but to follow
Meekly, with reverent steps, the sacred feet of her Saviour.
Thus many years she lived as a Sister of Mercy; frequenting
Lonely and wretched roofs in the crowded lanes of the city,
Where distress and want concealed themselves from the sunlight,—
Where disease and sorrow in garrets languished neglected.
Night after night, when the world was asleep, as the watchman re-
    peated
Loud through the gusty streets, that all was well in the city,
High at some lonely window he saw the light of her taper.
Day after day, in the gray of the dawn, as slow through the suburbs
Plodded the German farmer, with flowers and fruits for the market,
Met he that meek, pale face, returning home from its watchings.

  Then it came to pass that a pestilence fell on the city,
Presaged by wondrous signs, and mostly by flocks of wild pigeons,
Darkening the sun in their flight, with naught in their craws but an
    acorn.
And, as the tides of the sea arise in the month of September,
Flooding some silver stream, till it spreads to a lake in the meadow,
So death flooded life, and o'erflowing its natural margin,

Spread to a brackish lake, the silver stream of existence.
Wealth had no power to bribe, nor beauty to charm, the oppressor;
But all perished alike beneath the scourge of his anger:—
Only, alas! the poor, who had neither friends nor attendants,
Crept away to die in the almshouse, home of the homeless.
Then in the suburbs it stood, in the midst of meadows and wood-
       lands;—
Now the city surrounds it; but still, with its gateway and wicket
Meek, in the midst of splendor, its humble walls seem to echo
Softly the words of the Lord:—" The poor ye always have with you."
Thither, by night and by day, came the Sister of Mercy. The dying
Looked up into her face, and thought, indeed, to behold there
Gleams of celestial light encircle her forehead with splendor,
Such as the artist paints o'er the brows of saints and apostles,
Or such as hangs by night o'er a city seen at a distance.
Unto their eyes it seemed the lamps of the city celestial,
Into whose shining gates erelong their spirits would enter.

  Thus on a Sabbath morn, through the streets, deserted and silent,
Wending her quiet way, she entered the door of the almshouse.
Sweet on the summer air was the odor of flowers in the garden;
And she paused on her way to gather the fairest among them,
That the dying once more might rejoice in their fragrance and
      beauty.
Then, as she mounted the stairs to the corridors, cooled by the east-
      wind,
Distant and soft on her ear fell the chimes from the belfry of Christ
      Church,
While, intermingled with these, across the meadows were wafted
Sounds of psalms, that were sung by the Swedes in their church at
      Wicaco.
Soft as descending wings fell the calm of the hour on her spirit;
Something within her said, "At length thy trials are ended; "
And, with light in her looks, she entered the chambers of sickness.
Noiselessly moved about the assiduous, careful attendants,
Moistening the feverish lip, and the aching brow, and in silence
Closing the sightless eyes of the dead, and concealing their faces,
Where on their pallets they lay, like drifts of snow by the roadside.
Many a languid head, upraised as Evangeline entered,

Turned on its pillow of pain to gaze while she passed, for her presence
Fell on their hearts like a ray of the sun on the walls of a prison.
And, as she looked around, she saw how Death, the consoler,
Laying his hand upon many a heart, had healed it forever.
Many familiar forms had disappeared in the night-time;
Vacant their places were, or filled already by strangers.

  Suddenly, as if arrested by fear or a feeling of wonder,
Still she stood, with her colorless lips apart, while a shudder
Ran through her frame, and, forgotten, the flowerets dropped from
        her fingers
And from her eyes and cheeks the light and bloom of the morning.
Then there escaped from her lips a cry of such terrible anguish,
That the dying heard it and started up from their pillows.
On the pallet before her was stretched the form of an old man.
Long, and thin, and gray were the locks that shaded his temples;
But, as he lay in the morning light, his face for a moment
Seemed to assume once more the forms of its earlier manhood;
So are wont to be changed the faces of those who are dying,
Hot and red on his lips still burned the flush of the fever,
As if life, like the Hebrew, with blood had besprinkled its portals
That the Angel of Death might see the sign, and pass over.
Motionless, senseless, dying, he lay, and his spirit exhausted
Seemed to be sinking down through infinite depths in the darkness,
Darkness of slumber and death, forever sinking and sinking.
Then through those realms of shade, in multiplied reverberations,
Heard he that cry of pain, and through the hush that succeeded
Whispered a gentle voice, in accents tender and saint-like,
" Gabriel! O my beloved ! " and died away into silence.
Then he beheld, in a dream, once more the home of his childhood;
Green Acadian meadows, with sylvan rivers among them,
Village, and mountain, and woodlands; and, walking under their
        shadow,
As in the days of her youth, Evangeline rose in his vision.
Tears came into his eyes; and as slowly he lifted his eyelids,
Vanished the vision away, but Evangeline knelt by his bedside.
Vainly he strove to whisper her name, for the accents unuttered
Died on his lips, and their motion revealed what his tongue would
        have spoken.

Vainly he strove to rise; and Evangeline, kneeling beside him,
Kissed his dying lips, and laid his head on her bosom.
Sweet was the light of his eyes; but it suddenly sank into darkness.
As when a lamp is blown out by gust of wind at a casement.

All was ended now, the hope, and the fear, and the sorrow,
All the aching of heart, the restless, unsatisfied longing,
All the dull, deep pain, and constant anguish of patience!
And, as she pressed once more the lifeless head to her bosom
Meekly she bowed her own, and murmured, " Father, I thank thee ! "

———————

Still stands the forest primeval; but afar away from its shadow,
Side by side, in their nameless graves, the lovers are sleeping.
Under the humble walls of the little Catholic churchyard,
In the heart of the city, they lie, unknown and unnoticed.
Daily the tides of life go ebbing and flowing beside them.
Thousands of throbbing hearts, where theirs are at rest and forever,
Thousands of aching brains, where theirs no longer are busy,
Thousands of toiling hands, where theirs have ceased from their labors,
Thousands of weary feet, where theirs have completed their journey!
Still stands the forest primeval; but under the shade of its branches
Dwells another race, with other customs and language.
Only along the shore of the mournful and misty Atlantic
Linger a few Acadian peasants, whose fathers from exile
Wandered back to their native land to die in its bosom.
In the fisherman's cot the wheel and the loom are still busy;
Maidens still wear their Norman caps and their kirtles of homespun,
And by the evening fire repeat Evangeline's story,
While from its rocky caverns the deep-voiced, neighboring ocean
Speaks, and in accents disconsolate answers the wail of the forest.

www.ingramcontent.com/pod-product-compliance
Lightning Source LLC
Chambersburg PA
CBHW031506270326
41930CB00006B/280

*9 7 8 1 5 6 5 5 4 5 9 8 4 *